EXPLORING THE NEW TESTAMENT

EXPLORING THE
NEW
TESTAMENT

Walter M. Dunnett, Ph.D.

CROSSWAY BOOKS • WHEATON, ILLINOIS
A DIVISION OF GOOD NEWS PUBLISHERS

Exploring the New Testament

Copyright © 2001 by Evangelical Training Association

Published by Crossway Books
    a division of Good News Publishers
    1300 Crescent Street
    Wheaton, Illinois 60187

Previously published by Evangelical Training Association, 1963

Cover design: Cindy Kiple

First printing 2001

Printed in the United States of America

Unless otherwise noted, Scripture quotations are from the King James Version of the Bible.

Scripture references marked NASB are from the *New American Standard Bible®* Copyright © The Lockman Foundation 1960, 1962, 1963, 1968, 1971, 1972, 1973, 1975, 1977, 1995. Used by permission.

Scripture references marked ASV are from the *American Standard Version* of the Bible.

Library of Congress Cataloging-in-Publication Data
Dunnett, Walter M.
   [New Testament survey]
   Exploring the new testament / Walter M. Dunnett.
     p. cm.
   Originally published: Wheaton, Ill. : Evangelical Teacher Training Association, ©1963, in series: Broadening your biblical horizons.
   ISBN 1-58134-282-9 (pbk. : alk. paper)
   1. Bible N.T.—Introductions. I. Title.
BS2330.3 .D86   2001
225.6'1—dc21   2001002274
                                       CIP

15	14	13	12	11	10	09	08	07	06	05	04	03	02	01
15	14	13	12	11	10	9	8	7	6	5	4	3	2	1

CONTENTS

PREFACE

"Tell me, sir," the sincere young woman inquired anxiously of the preacher, "what is the Bible all about?" After serious thought the preacher replied, "My girl, the Bible is all about Jesus."

That, essentially, is the message of the New Testament. It is all about Jesus. From the story of the humble birth in Bethlehem as recorded in the Gospels, to the scene of the glorious exaltation as King of Kings and Lord of Lords depicted in the book of Revelation, the subject is the same. At the beginning of this study of the New Testament, the student will do well to look for the Lord Jesus Christ and His teachings.

Before a study of the books of the New Testament is undertaken in systematic fashion, two preliminary matters of great importance must be considered. The New Testament has a background which, when properly considered, will help to illuminate the books themselves. Chapter 1, therefore, deals with the three most important areas of this setting: the Hebrew, the Greek, and the Roman. Following this treatment, the chapter presents an overview, or "bird's-eye view," of the whole New Testament. This approach, sometimes called the "synthetic," is vital to acquaint the student with the major divisions or parts of the New Testament and the unity of the whole.

Having completed chapter 1, you, the student, are ready to investigate each book separately. Chapters 2 through 12 consider the respective writers and their writings—the purpose, outline, main content, and leading features.

The attention of the reader is called to the application activities at the end of each chapter and the bibliography at the end of the book. These serve at least a dual purpose: (1) They provide opportunity for you to carry on your studies in a more detailed and intensive manner whenever you wish to do so; (2) They provide information regarding matters that could be given only passing mention. You will find that the discussion questions at the end of the chapters will be valuable for testing your grasp of the materials you have studied.

Thanks are due to Moody Press, Chicago, for their kind permission given to use materials from my book, *An Outline of New Testament Survey*.

The outlines, charts, and one quotation in chapter 11 have been taken from that work.

On then to study. May it be done in the spirit of 2 Timothy 2:15 and result in the enrichment of the life of all who undertake the task at hand.

Walter M. Dunnett

BACKGROUND AND COMPOSITION OF THE NEW TESTAMENT

The world of the New Testament was a busy and exciting one. All roads led to Rome; the Caesars held sway across most of the inhabited earth; and in a tiny town of Palestine One was born who was to change the world! Following the time of Christ on earth, the Christian Church emerged, beginning as a small band of men and women, then growing to a great multitude of people. The books of the New Testament were written to instruct local congregations of believers and to inform them of the life and teachings of Christ.

But these events did not come about suddenly. They were the result of preparation—and that by God Himself! "But when the fulness of the time was come, God sent forth his Son" (Gal. 4:4). In the years that preceded the coming of Christ, God had been active in the lives of men and in the affairs of the nations. Many had a part in this pre-Christian era. Among the three most important contributors were the Hebrews and their religion, the Greeks and their language, and the Romans and their social and political organization.

THE HEBREW PREPARATION

Chosen by God as "a kingdom of priests, and an holy nation" (Ex. 19:6), the people of Israel were in a position of privilege. They were to be the messengers of the Lord to the nations around them. But they failed! Because of almost continuous disobedience and the gross sin of idolatry, God's judgment fell with finality upon them in the year 587 B.C., and the nation was carried away captive by Nebuchadnezzar into the land of Babylon.

From this center of captivity they were progressively scattered across the ancient world. This crucial event, called The Great Dispersion, left its effects upon the Hebrew people. But as they went, and wherever they went, many of them let it be known that they were worshipers of the one true God, Jehovah. Two emphases in particular, monotheism (the belief in only one God) and the Law of God, stood out in the midst of pagan societies.

In later years, when Christ was born and the apostolic proclamations went forth, the way had been prepared. The words, the ideas, the message itself was not entirely new. And not only had people heard the message, they had read it too. The Hebrew Old Testament was translated into Greek in the city of Alexandria in Egypt between the years 250-150 B.C. As Greek was then the common language of the world, this translation, called the Septuagint (meaning "the Seventy"), made the Old Testament teachings available to all who could read.

Sometime during the second century B.C., the major sects (or parties) among the Jews seem to have had their origin. As one reads the historical books of the New Testament (Matthew through Acts), the names of the Pharisees and the Sadducees often appear. The Pharisees were the larger of the two groups and were predominantly the students and teachers of the Old Testament, while the Sadducees were the powerful political leaders, including the high priests and leading officials of the Jerusalem Sanhedrin (composed of seventy people plus the high priest).

One is impressed with the orthodox character of the Pharisees. They firmly maintained the sacred character of the entire Old Testament, taught belief in the resurrection and the judgment of the last day, and affirmed the existence of angels and spirits. These tenets the Sadducees denied (Acts 23:6-8). Yet it was the former group that most often came under the condemnation of the Lord Jesus in His teaching—not because they failed to be orthodox, but because they emphasized the unimportant and neglected the weightier elements of the Law (Matt. 23:23, 24).

THE GREEK PREPARATION

One language and one world! That was the ambition of young Alexander, the son of King Philip of Macedon more than three hundred years before the birth of Christ. His ambition was largely realized between the years 334-323 B.C. Sweeping across the ancient world, like lightning across the sky, Alexander soon conquered much of the land. To cement his victories he established the Greek language as the *lingua franca*, the common tongue, and the Greek culture as the pattern of thought and life. Although his vast empire quickly disintegrated after his premature death, the results of that empire were long-standing.

How did these third-century happenings relate to the coming of

Christianity and the New Testament? A matchless vehicle of expression for the Christian message was provided. The apostolic preaching was done largely in Greek; and the New Testament books were written in Greek, the common language of the world. Using the vocabulary of their day, the writers filled the words with new and significant meaning designed to convey the message of spiritual life to their readers. Such important terms as *Christ, redeem, ransom, church, wisdom,* and *word* illustrate this.

THE ROMAN PREPARATION

Above all else Rome was noted for her insistence upon law and order. The world was organized into a great empire extending from the western end of the Mediterranean Sea to the Euphrates River in the Near East. By means of provinces and districts closely supervised by local governors, the empire was efficiently administered.

In the providence of God, the Romans prepared the world for the coming of Christianity in a number of ways.

First, the emphasis on law and order, backed by superior military might, made possible the days of peace during the reign of Caesar Augustus. It was during these days, says Luke the historian, that Mary brought forth her firstborn son (Luke 2:1-7) in the tiny village of Bethlehem in the Roman province of Judea.

Second, the Roman system of roads contributed greatly to the measure of ease and safety by which travelers could make their way back and forth across the empire. These roads were well paved, well drained, and usually patrolled. Paul traveled on such important roads as the Egnatian Way across Achaia and Macedonia and the Appian Way leading to Rome.

A thrid important factor, though negative in character, was the marked degeneration of morality and religion, and the deep longing for redemption found among the peoples of the Mediterranean Basin. They had lost faith in the ancient gods. The state religions were too formal and rigid to satisfy personal longings. The current philosophies of the day, likewise, lacked in real vigor and failed to appeal to the common man. Both in the East and the West, so-called mystery cults arose to offer personal salvation, fellowship with the gods, and the observance of secret rites.

Into this scene came Christianity proclaiming salvation, forgiveness, and peace. Centered in the historical incidents of the life, death, and resurrection of Jesus Christ, Christianity supplied the answer to man's spiritual need and moral void.

FIRST CENTURY PALESTINE

The principal ruling family in Palestine in the years that saw the dawn of the Christian era was the Herodian dynasty. Herod the Great was appointed by the Romans as the king of the Jews, reigning from 37 to 4 B.C. His rule was marked by intrigue and bloodshed, including the incident recorded in Matthew 2, called "the slaughter of the infants."

Of the sons of Herod the most noted in the gospel records was Herod Antipas who ruled from 4 B.C. to A.D. 39 as Tetrarch of Galilee and Perea. It was this Herod whom John the Baptist accused of wrongfully marrying Herodias, costing John his life (Matt. 14:1-12). Jesus called Herod "that fox" (Luke 13:32), and it was he who was involved in the trial of Christ in Jerusalem (Luke 23:7-12).

Herod Agrippa I, the son of Aristobulus and grandson of Herod the Great, succeeded Antipas and ruled over Galilee, Samaria, and Judea. His reign, from A.D. 37-44, was cut short by his sudden death. Acts 12 records his murder of James the son of Zebedee and the imprisonment of Peter together with a cryptic account of Herod's death (v. 21-23).

The last of the family to reign was Herod Agrippa II (A.D. 50-100). He appears in Acts 25 and 26 in conjunction with the trial of Paul before Festus in Caesarea. He, along with Festus, rendered a verdict of acquittal (26:31, 32).

Among the Roman procurators of Judea in the first century, Pontius Pilate (A.D. 26-36) is most notable as far as the New Testament record is concerned. Because of his share in the trial of Christ and his condemnation of the Lord after repeatedly rendering the verdict of "not guilty" (John 18:38–19:6), Pilate has attained unusual notoriety in history. Shortly after the death of Christ, he was deposed by Tiberius for an attack on the Samaritans and was ordered to appear before the emperor (A.D. 36). What actually happened to Pilate after this is uncertain.

Amid these political circumstances, the Jews were ruled directly by their own high priest and his cohorts in the Great Sanhedrin in Jerusalem. Three of these high priests are mentioned in the New Testament. Annas, the high priest emeritus, was the father-in-law to Caiaphas, the ruling high priest at the time of the trial of Christ (John 18:13); Ananias appears in Acts 23:2.

The religious life of the Jews was centered in the temple in Jerusalem. This structure, called Herod's Temple, was in process of completion during the time of Christ (cf. John 2:20). It had as its antecedents the temples of Solomon and Zerubbabel and was the symbol of their religious hopes and aspirations. From near and far the people came to worship, offer sacrifices, and observe the religious festivals of Judaism, especially the feasts of Passover, Pentecost, and Tabernacles.

Side by side with the temple in the religious life of Judaism was the synagogue. Especially to all those at a distance from Jerusalem, the synagogue was a substitute for the temple. There were a number of synagogues even in Jerusalem. They were primarily places of instruction and prayer for the Jews and Gentile adherents of the Jewish faith. The Scripture was read, commented on, and at various places in the service prayers were offered. Both Jesus and the early Christians frequented the synagogue (Luke 4:16-30; Acts 13:14ff.; 26:11).

To the Jew, the Old Testament was the book of God. God was One, the Law was the revelation of His will, and life was under His jurisdiction. There was an air of expectancy that God would intervene and save His people (Luke 2:25). So it was when Christ was born, He came into a world prepared—"in the fulness of the time." The New Testament complements the Old Testament, carrying on and completing the record of God's revelation, and clarifying to the Jew, the Gentile, and the Church of God the eternal truths of the living God.

COMPOSITION OF THE NEW TESTAMENT

The New Testament contains twenty–seven books that may be classified into three major groups based on their literary characteristics.

Chronological Division

Many scholars hold James to be the earliest book of the New Testament, written about A.D. 45.[1] Aside from the question of the place of James, it is practically certain that some of Paul's letters represent the first written records of the early church. Galatians is regarded by some to have been written as early as A.D. 47/48. The Thessalonian Epistles are from the early ministry of Paul the missionary, written from Corinth before or during the time of Gallio (cf. Acts 18:12-17; 1 Thess. 3:1-10), which would mean A.D. 50 or 51. These early writings give an insight into the character of the Christian message and Christians themselves. Especially important in this regard are passages such as Galatians 1:6–2:21; 6:11-17; 1 Thessalonians 1:2-10; 2:13-16; and 2 Thessalonians 2:1-12; 3:6-15.

In contrast to these writings, those of John the apostle constitute the last of the books to be written. According to tradition, as well as indications in the books themselves, John's works reflect problems being faced by the Church near the end of the first century. His major writings deal mainly with aspects of salvation: the Gospel—the nature of

salvation; the first epistle—the assurance of salvation; and the Revelation—the consummation of salvation.

Literary Division

While the literary divisions of the New Testament do not follow a
chronological scheme, they do reflect the logical order of God's program.
First, the Gospels and Acts constitute the basic history necessary for a
proper understanding and appreciation of the later works. The life of
Christ and the origin of the Church is foundational. The story of the
founder is required before one regards the superstructure that was
erected. The Church is "built upon the foundation of the apostles and
prophets, Jesus Christ himself being the chief corner stone" (Eph. 2:20).

Matthew—The introduction to "Jesus Christ, the King of the Jews."
Herein is recorded the fulfillment of many of the Old Testament prophecies with the coming of the Messiah. The teaching of Christ is emphasized.

Mark—The picture of Jesus as the "Servant of the Lord." He is busy
about His Father's work; thus Mark emphasizes the activity, especially
the redemptive activity, of Christ.

Luke—The portrait of Jesus as "the Son of Man," the perfect represen-
tative of humanity. His life was given "to seek and to save that which was
lost" (19:10). The sympathy and graciousness of Christ are emphasized.

John—The presentation of Jesus as the "the Son of God," the eternal Word who came to reveal God to man. This Gospel emphasizes the
relation of Christ to those around Him—the personal contacts that
changed the lives of those who met Him. By the true realization of His
divine Sonship, eternal life was received.

A Harmony of the Ministry of Jesus

Gospel	The Period of Preparation	The Period of Public Ministry		The Period of Suffering	The Period of Triumph
		Opening	Closing		
Matthew	1:1–4:16	4:17–16:20	16:21–26:2	26:3–27:66	28:1-20
Mark	1:1-13	1:14–8:30	8:31–13:37	14:1–15:47	16:1-20
Luke	1:1–4:13	4:14–9:21	9:22–21:38	22:1–23:56	24:1-53
John	1:1-34	1:35–6:71	7:1–12:50	13:1–19:42	20:1–21:25

Acts—This is the continuation of Luke's Gospel and presents the
risen Christ working through His apostles who had been empowered
by the Holy Spirit. The origin of the Church, the Body of Christ, and its

expansion "unto the uttermost part of the earth" is the theme of this first church history.

Second, the New Testament Epistles give the interpretation of the person and work of Christ and apply His teachings to the lives of believers. The majority of these letters, at least thirteen, were penned by the apostle Paul. Most of them are written in letter form. Of the twenty-one, all have names attached to them except Hebrews and the three Epistles of John.

Nine of the Pauline writings were sent to churches; four to individuals. Most of them deal with problem situations then existing in the churches (Ephesians seems to be an exception). Some are very personal in tone (Philippians and 2 Corinthians); others appear to have a more formal, almost thesis-like style, and in their main features (excluding the usual personal introduction and conclusion) show a rather businesslike tone. Romans would probably be the outstanding example of this type. Further, the letters of Paul show great variety in content, and also combine doctrinal and practical components in good balance.

The remaining epistles, while varied in authorship, may be conveniently grouped under two main headings. Some deal primarily with the problem of suffering (Hebrews, James, and 1 Peter), while the rest treat the problem of false teaching (2 Peter, 1, 2, and 3 John, and Jude). Both these problems became increasingly serious as the first century progressed. Persecution came first from Jewish opponents and later (after A.D. 64) from the Roman government. Christ had warned His followers of the rise of false Christs and false prophets (Matt. 24:24), and Paul had said much the same thing to the elders of the Ephesian church (Acts 20:29, 30). By the time John wrote his letters, the Gnostics (teachers who claimed to possess a superior philosophical-religious type of knowledge) were plaguing the Church. John's epistles were an answer to that error.

Finally, there is the well-known prophetical writing in the New Testament, the Revelation (or Apocalypse, the unveiling) of Jesus Christ. Like the prophecy of Daniel in the Old Testament, this book deals, for the most part, with the judgments of God in the last days upon "those that dwell upon the earth." In Revelation, the climax of redemption is portrayed. The earlier word of Paul, that God's purpose was "to sum up all things in Christ" (Eph. 1:10 ASV), is realized as John writes, "The kingdoms of this world are become *the kingdoms* of our Lord, and of his Christ; and he shall reign for ever and ever" (Rev. 11:15).

And so the New Testament has come to us. "God, who at sundry times and in divers manners spake in time past unto the fathers by the prophets, hath in these last days spoken unto us by *his* Son" (Heb.1:1, 2).

DISCUSSION QUESTIONS

1. Discuss the significant contributors and their contributions leading to the coming of Christ and the writing of the New Testament.
2. In what important ways did the Jewish Dispersion prepare the way for Christianity?
3. How did the Greek language and culture relate to Christianity?
4. In what ways did the Roman Empire contribute to the rise and spread of Christianity?
5. Distinguish between the Pharisees and the Sadducees. Which group is more prominent in the Gospels?
6. Name the three literary divisions of the New Testament and list the books included in each division.
7. Compare John's dealing with the subject of salvation in his Gospel, the first Epistle, and the Revelation.
8. How do the Gospels and the Acts lay the foundation for the remaining New Testament writings?
9. In what ways do the Epistles deal with the life and teachings of Christ?
10. How does the book of Revelation present Christ?

APPLICATION ACTIVITIES

1. To get a clearer view of Christ in the New Testament, prepare a simple chart to use throughout the class sessions, listing the various aspects of His character and work. For example:

Portraits of Christ

His Character	*His Work*
Model Sufferer, Luke 23:34	Savior, Luke 2:11
Sinless One, Luke 4	Teacher, Matthew 5

2. As the class sessions develop, list specific qualities in Christ's life desirable in your own life.
3. Refer to several good Bible commentaries or dictionaries for further background studies in preparation for a deeper understanding of the New Testament. In commentaries, background information is generally given prior to verse-by-verse comments.

THE SYNOPTIC GOSPELS

Matthew, Mark, Luke

The first three Gospels are called the Synoptic Gospels because they "see together" or have the same point of view with regard to the life of Christ. They present the life of Christ in a way that complements the picture given in the Gospel of John.

The approach to the subject here will be twofold: first, we will consider the distinctive features of each Gospel; second, we will look at the common features of the three Gospels. That is to say, what are the characteristics that cause each book to differ from the others and what are the common characteristics found in all three books?

THE GOSPEL OF MATTHEW

Author

Matthew, one of the original disciples of Christ, wrote the first book in the New Testament. He was first named Levi and worked as a publican collecting taxes in Palestine until he was called to follow Jesus (9:9, 10; Mark 2:14, 15).

Purpose and Content

Matthew addressed his Gospel primarily to Jewish readers and presented Jesus as the Messiah, the King of the Jews. This is seen in such passages as His genealogy (1:1-17); the visit of the Magi (2:1-12); His entry into Jerusalem (21:5); the judgment of the nations (25:31-46); and, in common with the other Gospels, the superscription over the Cross (27:37). In addition to these statements, there is much in this first Gospel concerning "the kingdom of heaven." This expression is used by Matthew alone.

This book also serves as the bridge between the Old and the New Testaments. It links together the prophecies of the coming Messiah with the fulfillment of prophecy in the person of the Lord Jesus. Matthew often alludes to or quotes from the prophets and connects their words with his subject. Of particular importance are such passages as 1:22, 23; 2:15, 17, 18, 23; 4:14, 16; 8:17; 12:17, 21; 21:4, 5; 26:54, 56; 27:9. It is as though Matthew first notes the Old Testament which says, "He is coming," then presents his own message which says, "He is here!"

The Discourses of Christ

The prominence of the discourses of Christ is easily observed in this Gospel. Matthew's pattern, as may be seen clearly in the outline of the book, is to include narrative material about Christ. Then follows an important discourse. There are five in the book, one in each of the five major divisions:

1. The Sermon on the Mount (5:1–7:29)
2. The Commission to the Twelve (10:1-42)
3. The Parables of the Kingdom (13:1-53)
4. The Meaning of Greatness and Forgiveness (18:1-35)
5. The Olivet Discourse (24:1–25:46)

In one way or another, each of these discourses relates to the claims that the King makes upon those who would share in His kingdom.

Outline

In the light of the dominant theme of this Gospel, then, the following outline will aid the student's progress through the book. The clue to Matthew's structure is given by the fivefold repetition of the expression "when Jesus had finished [or *ended* or *made an end of*]" (7:28; 11:1; 13:53; 19:1; 26:1). This phrase marks the end of each major division of the Gospel. Together with the introduction (1:1–4:11) and the two concluding sections (26:3–28:15; 28:16-20), these five divisions form the complete record.

The introduction of the King	1:1–4:11
The demands of the King	4:12–7:29
The deeds of the King	8:1–11:1
The program of the King	11:2–13:53
The destiny of the King	13:54–19:2
The problems of the King	19:3–26:2
The death and resurrection of the King	26:3–28:15
The final commission by the King	28:16-20

THE GOSPEL OF MARK

Author

In contrast to Matthew, Mark was not one of the original disciples of Christ. He was, however, a native of Jerusalem (Acts 12:12), a companion of Simon Peter (1 Peter 5:13), and the cousin of Barnabas (Col. 4:10) who, in turn, was a close associate of Paul and the Jerusalem apostles. His relationship to the apostles was, therefore, close enough to render him familiar with the life of Christ and the activities of the early Christian group.

In A.D. 112, Papias cited Mark as "the interpreter of Peter." A comparison of Peter's sermon in Acts 10:34-43 with Mark's Gospel shows the former to be an outline of the life of Jesus that Mark has given much greater detail.

Purpose and Content

Mark addressed his Gospel primarily to Roman readers and presented Jesus as the Worker, the Servant of Jehovah. (According to tradition, Mark wrote his record of the life of Christ in Rome.) The chief characteristic of Christ in this book is His activity, the mark of a good servant. The Greek word *eutheos*, translated variously as "straightway," "immediately," "anon," or "forthwith," appears forty-two times in the book. This message made a natural appeal to the busy, practical Roman reader.

According to the amount of space Mark allots to it, the most important activity of Christ was His death and resurrection. About three-eighths of the entire book is devoted to the narrative of the Passion Week (the last week of the life of Christ, 11:1–16:18). In the story, this is the most striking feature and shows clearly what aspect of Christ's life was considered by the Gospel writers to be of supreme concern.

Outline

In keeping with the theme of the activity of Christ, the outline treats His life as a series of tours as He carried on His ministry. By so doing, one is impressed with the continual busyness of the Servant of Jehovah.

Introduction	1:1
Preparatory events	1:2-13
First tour of Galilee—Miracles and parables	1:14–4:34
Tour of Decapoli	4:35–5:43
Second tour of Galilee	6:1-29
Retreat to the desert	6:30-52
Third tour of Galilee	6:53–7:23
Tour of the north country	7:24–9:29
First announcement of passion	8:31
Fourth tour of Galilee	9:30-50
Second announcement of passion	9:31

Tour of Perea and Judea	10:1-52
Third announcement of passion	10:33
Ministry in Jerusalem	11:1–13:37
The passion and resurrection	14:1–16:20

THE GOSPEL OF LUKE

Author

According to the New Testament, Luke was a physician (Col. 4:14), a companion of Paul (Philem. 24), and the writer of a two-volume history of the life of Christ and the early church (Luke and Acts). His Gospel has long been the favorite of Christian and non-Christian readers alike because of its sublime presentation of a spotless life. Luke, as Mark, was not among the original disciples of Christ.

Purpose and Content

Luke addressed his Gospel primarily to Greek (or non-Jewish) readers and presented Jesus as the Son of Man, the ideal human being. As the Greeks had long sought after the "perfect man," Luke's work was designed to fulfill that quest. Some of the most important passages are the account of the birth of Christ (1:26-38; 2:8-20); the testimony of God to His Son (3:21, 22); the announcement of Jesus as the Anointed One (4:16-24); and the mission of the Son of Man (19:10). Together with these passages one should consider Luke's emphasis on the prayers of Jesus; His matchless parables (10:30-37; 15:1-32; 18:9-14); the human interest features (10:38-42; 19:1-10; 24:13-35) where the Lord deals graciously yet firmly with interesting people; and the prominence of the Holy Spirit in the life of Christ (1:35; 3:22; 4:1, 18).

A further illustration of the outreach of this book is the repetition of phrases having relation to humanity. From first to last, Luke shows that the Gospel (God's Good News) is meant for all men (2:10, 14, 31, 32; 3:6; 9:56; 10:33; 17:16; 19:10; 24:47).

Outline

The outline is based upon the concept of Christ as "the Son of Man." Luke portrays Him as carrying on a full ministry among the peoples of Palestine with a view to the extension of that ministry to the regions beyond (24:47; cf. Acts 1:8).

Prologue—The purpose stated	1:1-4
The preparation of the Son of Man	1:5–4:13
The Galilean ministry of the Son of Man	4:14–9:50
The Perean ministry of the Son of Man	9:51–18:30

The Jerusalem ministry of the Son of Man	18:31–21:38
The passion ministry of the Son of Man	22:1–23:56
The resurrection ministry of the Son of Man	24:1-53

CHARACTERISTICS COMMON TO THE GOSPELS

While each Gospel has its distinctive emphasis, a number of great events or areas are common to them all. This fact has made these among the best known teachings and events of Christ's ministry:

Announcement of the Savior by John the Baptist (Matt. 3; Mark 1; Luke 3)

Baptism of the Savior (Matt. 3; Mark 1; Luke 3)

Temptation of the Savior (Matt. 4; Mark 1; Luke 4)

Teachings and Miracles of the Savior (the major portion of each Gospel)

Transfiguration of the Savior (Matt. 17; Mark 9; Luke 9)

Trial, Death, and Burial of the Savior (Matt. 26, 27; Mark 14, 15; Luke 22, 23)

Resurrection of the Savior (Matt. 28; Mark 16; Luke 24)

OTHER SPECIAL FEATURES

In addition, the narrative of Christ's birth and certain events in His life are given in detail.

Unusual Nature of Christ's Birth

Emphasis is placed upon the unusual nature of Christ's birth—it was prophesied in the Old Testament, announced by an angel to Joseph and Mary, and brought about by the operation of the Holy Spirit (Matt. 1, 2; Luke 1, 2).

The Parables of Christ

The teachings and miracles of Christ occupy the major portion of the gospel records. Distinctive in His teachings was the frequent use of parables. A parable is a story or situation in the human realm which is employed as a means of illustrating or defending some spiritual principle. In these three Gospels at least thirty separate parables are found, plus many other short, axiomatic statements that are parabolic in nature. Among the most notable of these are the parables of the kingdom in Matthew 13 and the parables of the lost things in Luke 15.

The Kingdom

One of the most important areas of our Lord's teaching was concerned with the kingdom. The two expressions, "the kingdom of heaven" and "the kingdom of God," occur often, although the former is limited to Matthew. God's kingdom is essentially "His rule over His creation." It is first of all, a spiritual reality. "The kingdom of God cometh not with observation . . . for, behold, the kingdom of God is within you" (Luke 17:20, 21). The kingdom is in the hearts of believers, but it is also a visible reality. The Son of Man "shall come in his glory . . . and before him shall be gathered all nations" (Matt. 25:31, 32). At this time He shall appear and rule over the earth, a theme so prevalent in the prophets (cf. Isa. 11:1-10; Zech.13:1-6; Mal. 4:1-3). When the kingdom was announced by John the Baptist (Matt. 3:1-3) and by the Lord Jesus (Mark 1:14, 15), the spiritual aspect was prominent. In the coming of "the Day of the Lord" at the close of this age, the visible aspect will be evidenced. Thus God's program will be fulfilled, all things will be summed up in Christ, and ultimately God will be all in all.

The Miracles

Alongside His teachings, the miracles of Christ formed an important part of His ministry. They were both evidences of His messiahship and occasions for bringing needy people to a realization of a greater need than physical necessities—that of spiritual need. In proportion to its length, more miracles are found in Mark than in Matthew and Luke—at least twenty individual situations. This is quite in keeping with Mark, the Gospel of the busy Servant. When the Lord formally announces Himself as God's Anointed at the outset of His public ministry (Luke 4:16-21), He included these two aspects of His commission: the proclamation of the Gospel and the working of miracles. When He had thus announced Himself, He added, "This day is this Scripture fulfilled in your ears" (v. 21). Both His words and His works were means of revealing God to men. This was the function of the Son (Matt. 11:27).

DISCUSSION QUESTIONS

1. What is meant by the "Synoptic Gospels?"
2. To whom was each of the Synoptic Gospels written and for what purpose?
3. Summarize the distinctive content of each book.
4. Give at least one important biographical fact about each of the writers of these three Gospels. Illustrate by a Scripture reference for each.
5. Discuss the unique position of the book of Matthew as linking the Old and New Testaments.
6. State the five major discourses of Christ in the book of Matthew.

7. How is the activity of Christ made prominent in Mark?
8. In Luke's Gospel, what are some ways in which Jesus is portrayed as the Son of Man?
9. What common characteristics are found in all three books?
10. What are the distinctive characteristics of each book?

APPLICATION ACTIVITIES

1. Prepare your own outline of each Synoptic Gospel.
2. For a fuller comprehension of the Synoptic Gospels, prepare a simply-diagramed chart showing the important features of each, such as main theme, persons, parables, miracles, and teachings.
3. From your study in Activity #2, note the progression of opposition against Christ. Where did this opposition begin? Where did it end? What type of people were usually the instigators of opposition? What were the issues?
4. Summarize Christ's prophetic teachings presented in His Olivet Discourse.

GOSPEL OF JOHN

Author

According to the persistent tradition of the Church since the early second century, the fourth Gospel was written by John the apostle, son of Zebedee and brother of James. As one of the Twelve, he was close to Jesus. He is usually identified with the beloved disciple who appears anonymously a number of times in this book (13:23; 18:15, 16; 19:26, 27).

Purpose and Content

John clearly states his purpose for writing this Gospel (20:30, 31), placing emphasis upon three important words: *signs, believe,* and *life.* A good understanding of these terms, together with their use in the Gospel, allows one to gain a working knowledge of the book's content.

Signs

The word *signs* is John's term for the miracles of Jesus.[1] By it he means to impress the reader with the meaning of the miracle and especially with the revelation of who Jesus really is. Taken together, the signs are meant to show that Jesus is "the Christ, the Son of God."

Out of the many signs which Jesus did, John selected seven to demonstrate the nature of Christ. Each of them has a particular message.

1. Water changed into wine—Jesus' power over *quality*
2. The nobleman's son healed—Jesus' power over *distance*
3. The impotent man healed—Jesus' power over *time*
4. The five thousand fed—Jesus' power over *quantity*
5. Walking on the water—Jesus' power over *natural law*
6. The blind man healed—Jesus' power over *helplessness*
7. Lazarus raised from the dead—Jesus' power over *death*

Of the seven signs, five are found only in John's Gospel. The feeding of the five thousand is the only miracle recorded by all the writers; the walking on the water appears also in Matthew and Mark.

Believe

One of the most frequent words in the book, *believe*, appears at least ninety-eight times. It always occurs in the verb form, never the noun form (*believe*, never *belief*). This continually gives the impression of action, of something happening. John is teaching the meaning of believing in Jesus not so much by definition as by illustration. The word is used to indicate the response of people to Jesus. If they believed on Him, they became His followers; if they did not believe, they became His opponents. At any rate, once having met Him, they could not remain neutral.

Along with the word *believe*, John employs a number of synonyms to make his meaning clear. Some of these are *receive* (1:12), *drink* (4:14), *come* (6:35), *eat* (6:51), and *enter* (10:9). All these words, used in the routine of daily life, become full with meaning when applied to the spiritual relationship of men and women to Christ. Believing on Him is like receiving a gift, drinking refreshing water, entering by a door into a sheepfold. The need is met, the thirst is quenched, the hunger is satiated.

Life

This term expresses the result of believing in Christ. To receive life is to become a child of God by being born into His family. It is the divine nature imparted to the believer. The Lord Jesus said to the Pharisee, Nicodemus: "Except a man be born again, he cannot see the kingdom of God" (3:3). This life is described as eternal in quality (3:15) and is, therefore, the opposite of the state of spiritual death, which means to perish (3:16).

In addition, there will be a manifestation of this gift in the one who receives it. The Holy Spirit, who is the agent of regeneration, will be as rivers of living water flowing from within the one who has drunk of the water of life (7:37-39). Thus the life is imparted to others around the believer, as dry ground is refreshed by a stream.

Thus, John has stated his purpose. In writing the story of Christ, he has sought to bring his readers face to face with this person who by His words and His works confronts men and women with a great decision. From first to last Christ is described as deity (1:1; 20:28). Yet He has come in human form (1:14) so that He might give Himself to bring life to those who sit in the shadow of death (12:23, 24). Not only did Christ die, but He rose again (chap. 20). As the living Lord, He calls forth the devotion and loyalty of His followers (21:15-19).

Outline

Christ's Teachings

Having gained a general idea of what John has done in writing his Gospel, let us consider the teachings of the Lord Jesus. What does He teach and how does He impart these truths to the people?

The relationship between the signs and His teaching

The signs were occasions for Jesus' teaching, so that one may expect to find this order followed in the book.

In chapter 5, Jesus healed the infirm man beside the pool of Bethesda in Jerusalem. Following the sign, the Jews challenged His right to do such a thing on the Sabbath Day (5:16). This called forth His claims of equality with God in nature (5:17, 18), in power (5:21), and in authority (5:26, 27). To substantiate these claims, He called upon certain witnesses including John the Baptist (5:33), His own works (5:36), the Father (5:37), the Scriptures (5:39), and Moses (5:46).

In chapter 6, Jesus was faced with the task of feeding more than five thousand hungry people. After His disciple Philip had failed to provide a solution to the problem, Andrew brought a boy to Jesus with his lunch of five barley loaves and two fishes (6:9). Using these, Jesus fed the people and thus met their physical need (6:12). When the crowd returned the following day, obviously looking for another free meal, the Lord admonished them to "labour not for the meat which perisheth" (6:27). Then He taught them of their spiritual need and declared, "I am the bread of life" (6:35). A lengthy discourse followed in which He drew a contrast between "the flesh" and "the spirit" (6:63). He uncovered the shortcomings in their understanding of spiritual realities.

They held improper motives (6:26). In coming to Him only for physical bread, they had missed the meaning of the sign. They employed improper methods (6:28), failing to do the works of God. They retained an improper conception of their religious heritage (6:30, 31), placing Christ on the same level as Moses. They evidenced an improper desire in asking for this bread (6:34). For when He explained what it meant "to eat the living bread," they murmured, strove one with another (6:52), and, finally, many who followed Him turned away (6:66).

In addition to these two outstanding examples, the sign of chapter 9 is an admirable illustration of His claim, "I am the light of the world" (8:12; 9:5), and the sign of chapter 11 makes clear His claim, "I am the resurrection and the life" (11:25).

The seven "I am's"

The Lord Jesus makes claims for Himself by means of the "I am" phrases in this Gospel. Although some of these have been referred to in passing, the complete list should be carefully observed by the reader:

1. "I am the bread of life" (6:35)
2. "I am the light of the world" (8:12; 9:5)
3. "I am the door" (10:7, 9)
4. "I am the good shepherd" (10:11)
5. "I am the resurrection and the life" (11:25)
6. "I am the way, the truth, and the life" (14:6)
7. "I am the true vine" (15:1)

Aside from the graphic figures Christ employed to describe Himself, the striking thing about these claims is their exclusive nature. In the Greek, "I am" is an emphatic grammatical construction. The Lord states to the Jews, "Verily, verily, I say unto you, before Abraham was, I am" (8:58). He thus took upon Himself the title of deity from their Old Testament Scriptures, for this was the title by which God revealed Himself to Moses (Ex. 3:14). The alternative to eating "the bread of life" is death; if one refuses "the light," he remains in darkness. He is "the only way;" no one comes to God except by Him. He is the "true vine," not an imitation.

The personal interview

Of great importance in communicating his message is John's use of personal interviews. Again and again, people are brought into contact with Jesus. They are never the same again. Either they believe and follow Him, or they turn away in unbelief. While there are many such situations in the book, the main examples include:

Andrew—Though Andrew was not as well-known as his brother Simon Peter, he possessed noteworthy qualities. Andrew, having believed in Jesus for himself, became a personal worker. He is always seen bringing someone else to Jesus. First, his brother, Simon; then a lad; then the Greek visitors in Jerusalem (1:35-42; 6:8, 9; 12:20-22).

Simon Peter—When Peter met Jesus, the prophecy of his new name (meaning a change in character) was given. He was Simon (meaning unstable); he would become Cephas (meaning "a stone;" 1:42). Along with this he was ready to confess his faith in Jesus as "the Son of the living God" (6:68, 69). Although he was overconfident, leading to his temporary denial of his Lord (13:36-38; 18:15-18, 25-27), he was graciously restored and recommissioned to follow Christ anew and feed His sheep (21:15-22).

Nicodemus—Although Nicodemus was a man thoroughly trained in the Old Testament truths, he had not experienced the new birth; he did not have a realization of the messiahship of Jesus. The Lord explained for Nicodemus how He himself fulfilled the Old Testament type of the serpent in the wilderness, and how as God's Son He was sent to be the Savior of all who would believe in Him (3:1ff.). That Nicodemus came to true belief seems to be indicated by the incidents that follow in the book (7:50, 51; 19:39-42).

Using the same approach, the following people in John's Gospel are worthy of study:

Philip (1:43-46; 6:5-7; 14:8-12)

The woman of Samaria (4:1-42)

The blind man (chap. 9)

Martha and Mary (11:1-46)

Thomas—In him is seen the culmination of belief in John's Gospel with his confession of the deity of Christ—"my Lord and my God" (11:16; 14:5-7; 20:24-28).

Pilate—He is the outstanding example of unbelief in the Gospel (18:28–19:16), along with Judas Iscariot (6:70, 71; 13:21-30; 18:1-15).

Upper Room Discourse

Attention should be given to the unique discourse of this Gospel found in chapters 13-16, commonly called the Upper Room Discourse. Bishop B. F. Westcott calculated that 92 percent of the material in John was unique and that, consequently, only 8 percent was material held in common with the Synoptic Gospels. Of John's unique material, this section is the most outstanding unit in the book. After His public ministry was concluded (at the end of chap. 12), Jesus met privately with His disciples and told them of two important things that were soon to happen. First, His departure was near. He was going away; they could not come with Him at this point. Eventually, however, He would return to receive them into the Father's house. Second, the Holy Spirit would be sent to take His place. He would not leave the disciples alone (literally "orphans," 14:18, NASB). He would send "another Comforter," one "just like Himself." The Holy Spirit would indwell them (14:17), teach them (14:26), empower them to witness (15:26, 27), and guide them into all the truth (16:13).

Prologue and Epilogue

Finally, notice the opening and closing sections of the book, the prologue (1:1-18) and the epilogue (21:1-25). The former contains the message of the entire Gospel. In the prologue, John introduces: (1) The chief character of the book—*the Word.* The Word is God, the Creator, the Giver of Life, the One manifest in flesh, and the Revealer of the Father. (2) The chief vocabulary terms of the book—*life, light, darkness, witness, believe, truth.* (3) The chief plot of the book—conflict. Notice the words used to illustrate spiritual conflict: light vs. darkness; received him not vs. received him; physical birth vs. spiritual birth; law vs. grace and truth. This conflict continues throughout the book until it culminates in the cross and the resurrection.

The epilogue furnishes an appropriate climax to the Gospel. It teaches the logical result of believing in Jesus. True believers will follow Jesus and thus give expression to their faith in service (21:19). Peter learned that believing in Jesus did not only eventuate in the spoken word of confession, but in the life of dedicated service.

Discussion Questions

1. Define and show the importance of each of the three words: *signs, believe, life.*
2. What is the striking feature about the "I am" claims of Christ? Illustrate this from Scripture.
3. What two important messages were communicated in the Upper Room Discourse?
4. What is the contribution of the prologue to the message of John?
5. What does the epilogue of the book emphasize?

APPLICATION ACTIVITIES

1. Trace the Scriptures in John that reveal Christ's deity.
2. List and summarize the passages in John referring to the Holy Spirit.
3. In John's Gospel, list Christ's various titles and their significance.
4. Using the chart idea suggested in chapter 2, activity #2, trace events in Christ's life as recorded in John's Gospel. What is the significance of John's writing of events that are not included in the other three Gospels?

BOOK OF ACTS

This is the second volume of Luke's history of Christianity. Without the book of Acts, many details of the life of the early church would be missing. Of the first thirty years we would know only what could be pieced together from the New Testament Epistles.

From the book of Acts itself we discover that Luke, the author, was a companion of Paul and an eyewitness to many of the events about which he writes. This evidence appears in the so-called "we sections" of the text, that is, places where Luke includes himself in the story by the use of the first person plural pronoun (16:10-17; 20:5–21:18; 27:1–28:16). Besides Luke's firsthand experiences, he also had occasions for personal interviews. Paul was able to tell him of his Gentile ministry; the leaders at Jerusalem proved to be valuable resources concerning the Jerusalem church; and Philip in Caesarea gave him access to the data of Philip's Samaritan ministry.

Purpose

Why did Luke write the book of Acts? What were the chief motives behind his work? Consider the following:

The historical motive

This is the most obvious one, of course. Acts is a continuation of the narrative begun in the Gospel of Luke (Luke 1:1-4; cf. Acts 1:1-5). The books are addressed to the same individual, Theophilus. They are linked together by the phrase, "the former treatise." One concerns what "Jesus began both to do and teach," while the other records the continuation of that ministry by "the apostles whom he had chosen."

Again, compare Luke 24:44-53 with Acts 1:6-11. Both passages speak of the coming of the Holy Spirit, of the disciples as witnesses, and of the ascension of the Lord Jesus into heaven.

Luke, therefore, gives his readers the history of the first sixty or sixty-five years of Christianity. About thirty years were included in each of his two works. It is the story of the Good News of salvation, beginning in a manger in Bethlehem and extending to the very hub of the Empire, of Rome itself (cf. Phil. 4:22). The narrative opens with the witness of the shepherds in the fields of Judea and terminates with the salutations of saints in Caesar's household.

The doctrinal motive

As in his Gospel, Luke's chief doctrinal emphasis here is upon the person and work of the Holy Spirit. In fact, the explicit references to the Spirit in Acts occur with great frequency (Acts 1-11; 13, 15, 16, 19, 20, 21, and 28). The Lord Jesus, in His last recorded utterance prior to the Ascension, promised the disciples that "ye shall receive power, after that the Holy Ghost is come upon you." The fulfillment of that promise is clearly seen in the Acts. The Holy Spirit was the motivating power in the apostles' witness and work for Christ. The Spirit filled them again and again (cf. 2:4; 4:8, 31; 6:5; 7:55; 9:17; 11:24; 13:9). In situations where discipline (5:3, 4), wisdom (6:3), or guidance (16:6, 7) was required, the Holy Spirit operated in the believers. By His coming, differing groups were united into that one great company, the Church (the Jews, chap. 2; the Samaritans, chap. 8; the Gentiles, chap. 10; some disciples of John, chap. 19).

The apologetic motive

In one sense, the book of Acts is simply a defense of Christianity. That believers need to defend (1 Peter 3:15; Phil. 1:17-18) and contend for the faith is clear (Jude 3). Luke shows to the world that in the first generation, the Church was never the object of official persecution at the hands of the Roman government—the Jews, often; but the Romans, never. This is a remarkable record which, at that particular time when Paul had appealed to Caesar for a fair trial, needed to be clearly stated.

In each contact between the apostles and officials of the Roman government, they were either accepted or ignored but never persecuted. A number of these situations are recorded by Luke:

1. Paul and Barnabas before Sergius Paulus, the proconsul at Cyrus—he "believed" (Acts 13).

2. Paul and Silas in Philippi—The Roman jailer was saved, and the magistrates of this Roman colony apologized for the unjust treatment accorded the missionaries because of the false charges of the Jews (Acts 16).

3. Paul before Gallio, the proconsul of Achaia—He "cared for none of these things" (i.e., problems of Jewish law, Acts 18); Gallio was indifferent.

4. Paul in Ephesus—The Asiarchs (Acts 19:31) were friends of Paul; the town clerk restored order, thereby rescuing the missionaries from possible violence.

5. Paul safeguarded by Claudius Lysias, the Roman captain of the castle Antonia in Jerusalem (Acts 21, 22).

6. Paul before Felix in Caesarea—He often called for and listened to Paul speak (Acts 24).

7. Paul before Festus in Caesarea—He considered Paul innocent of the charges against him by the Jews (Acts 25).

When persecution against the apostles and the Church does appear in Acts, it is at the hands of the Jews—either the Sanhedrin or groups such as those who follow Paul in his journeys (cf. chaps. 4, 5, 7, 8, 16, 17, 18) and the silversmiths of Ephesus (Acts 19).

The biographical motive

Of the many interesting and important persons who appear in Acts, Peter and Paul are those to whom Luke gives a place of prominence. His record is concentrated largely upon their activities. Peter occupies the major portion of chapters 1-12; Paul of chapters 13-28.

It might be said that the first generation of the Church was the story of these two. The Jerusalem church was led by Peter for the first few years of its existence. Even the early probing into surrounding areas, such as Samaria (chap. 8) and Caesarea (chap. 10), were to one degree or another the work of Peter. The ministry of the Gospel in the Gentile lands, from Syria to Rome itself, was mainly carried on by Paul. In the great provinces of Galatia, Macedonia, Achaia, and Asia, he founded churches and established them in their newfound faith.

Working alongside Peter and Paul were a number of other notable individuals: Stephen (chap. 6, 7); Philip the evangelist (chap. 8); Barnabas (chap. 4, 9, 11, 13-15); John Mark (chap. 12, 13, 15); Silas (chap.15-17); Timothy (chap. 16, 17); Aquila and Priscilla (chap. 18); Apollos (chap. 18, 19). Some of these and others as well also appear in Paul's epistles, where they are described as his fellow workers.

In giving this record, then, Luke has made it clear which people were actively responsible for the growth and expansion of the Church. Thus the epistles are illuminated for us by his biographical portraits.

Outline

The key verse of Acts, chapter one verse eight, provides a basis for the outline of the book. As the Lord Jesus spoke of the future ministry to be accomplished by His followers, consequent upon the coming of the

Holy Spirit, He stressed two things: (1) persons and (2) places. "Ye shall be witnesses unto me"—that is the personnel of the mission. "In Jerusalem, and in all Judea, and in Samaria, and unto the uttermost part of the earth"—that is the geography of the mission. The main divisions of the outline reveal the primary locations; the subpoints indicate the chief persons in each place.

Introduction—Apostolic commission given	1:1-11
The Gospel in Jerusalem—Origins	1:12–8:3
The ministry of Peter	1:12–5:42
The ministry of Stephen	6:1–8:3
The Gospel in Samaria and Judea—Transition	8:4–11:18
The ministry of Philip	8:4-40
The ministry of Saul begun	9:1-31
The ministry of Peter concluded	9:32–11:18
The Gospel in the uttermost part—Expansion	11:19–21:14
The ministry of Barnabas	11:19–12:25
The ministry of Paul the apostle	13:1–21:14
The first journey	13:1–14:28
The Jerusalem Council	15:1-35
The second journey	15:36–18:22
The third journey	18:23–21:14
The Gospel in Caesarea and Rome—Imprisonment	21:15–28:29
Paul taken prisoner in Jerusalem	21:15–23:10
Paul as a prisoner in Caesarea	23:11–26:32
Paul as a prisoner in Rome	27:1–28:29
Conclusion—Apostolic commission fulfilled	28:30, 31

The Gospel in Jerusalem

In the first section of Acts, it is Peter who plays a part in a variety of situations. He assumes the leadership after the Ascension of the Lord and is instrumental in bringing about the election of Matthias after Judas Iscariot's suicide. Peter preaches the notable sermon on the Day of Pentecost resulting in the salvation of three thousand persons. He and John heal the lame man at the temple gate and subsequently defend their act and preaching before the Jewish Sanhedrin. It is Peter who condemns Ananias and Sapphira for their plot to deceive the church and leads the congregation in the choice of the seven to supervise the distribution of goods to the widows.

One thing that is outstanding throughout this narrative is the spirit of unity that prevailed among the Christians. Notice carefully the references that illustrate this condition, especially the first prayer meeting (1:14); the preparation for Pentecost (2:1); the sharing of goods and consistent witness (2:43-47; 4:23-31); the prayer for boldness (4:23-31); the daily ministry of the Word (5:41, 42).

Near the end of the opening unit, Stephen is featured as a mighty and fearless defender of the faith. While he loses his life, becoming the first martyr of the Church, his influence endures. This is especially important in the case of one of the spectators at his martyrdom, a young man named Saul (7:58), who later is brought to Christ and becomes Paul the apostle. At this point, however, he sets out to persecute the believers and forces them all, except the apostles, to flee from Jerusalem.

The Gospel in Judea and Samaria

The second major section of the book concerns the work of the Church in the regions of Judea and Samaria, just to the north of Jerusalem. Philip the evangelist, one of the seven chosen in chapter 6, went to Samaria, and the result was most gratifying. Many believed his message concerning Christ. When the church in Jerusalem heard the news, Peter and John were sent to confirm them in their newfound faith (Acts 8:15-17). Philip departed to the south, near Gaza, and led the Ethiopian treasurer to Christ. Peter went on toward the seacoast, eventually coming to the home of Cornelius, the Roman centurion in Caesarea, and had the joy of witnessing the salvation of Cornelius and those of his household. With the reception of the Holy Spirit, these Gentile believers were recognized as sharing in the fellowship of the Church with the Jews (chap. 2) and the Samaritans (chap. 8).

During this period of history, the conversion of Saul occurs (chap. 9). That Luke attaches great importance to this event is evidenced by his three long accounts of the incident (cf. chaps. 9, 22, 26). With Paul's conversion, the chief persecutor of the Church is changed into her most prominent defender and preacher.

The Gospel to the Uttermost

The third and most lengthy unit of Acts is mainly the record of the development and expansion of the Gentile ministry led by Paul and his fellow workers.[1] Going back to the record of Saul's persecution of the church in Jerusalem (cf. 11:19 with 8:1-4), Luke first traces the progress of the Gospel from the home base to the Syrian city of Antioch. Here the narrative resumes with the dispatching of Barnabas to establish the new believers in that important city. Antioch, ranked as the third city of the Empire (after Rome and Alexandria), became the home base for missionary work among the Gentiles. After Barnabas went to Tarsus and brought Saul back with him, the two worked together in the church until it was thriving. It was here that believers were first called Christians (11:26). Then, following a brief trip to Jerusalem to deliver needed goods to the famine-stricken Christians, these two men were called by the Holy Spirit to a new and larger work—and the missionary journeys of Paul began.

"The Missionary Journeys of Paul" chart in the back of the book will make clear the particulars of Paul's ventures.

The Journeys of Paul

The initial journey was concentrated primarily in the province of Galatia (chaps. 13-15); the second in the province of Macedonia and Achaia (chaps. 16-18); the third in the province of Asia (chaps. 19-20).[2] In these places, Paul spent most of his time in population centers—cities like Antioch of Pisidia, Philippi, Thessalonica, Corinth, and Ephesus. Once the evangelization of these cities had been completed, the Gospel radiated to the surrounding country (cf. 1 Thess. 1:8).

Paul found himself in a variety of situations and audiences. On occasion the missionary was in the Jewish synagogue (as in Pisidian Antioch, Thessalonica, Athens, Corinth, and Ephesus); or before the leaders of the city (as in Athens); or in prison (as in Philippi). When preaching to a Jewish audience, Paul used the Old Testament Scriptures as a basis for his message (as in Antioch and Thessalonica); whereas in addressing pagan, or at least non-Jewish groups, he generally began with their natural surroundings (as in Lystra and Athens). His usual approach was to preach first to the Jews of the region, if they were to be found; then to the Gentiles.

Paul's ministry in these areas, covering a period of about ten years, resulted in the establishment of a chain of churches all along the Mediterranean shores. As he wrote to the Roman Christians, he recalled that "from Jerusalem, and round about unto Illyricum, I have fully preached the gospel of Christ" (Rom. 15:19). This period of his labors was terminated with the final visit to Jerusalem which resulted in his arrest (on a false charge by some Asian Jews) and his consequent imprisonments, both in Caesarea and Rome.

The final section of Acts is the record of Paul's experiences while a prisoner. He makes his defense before a Jewish mob and the Jewish leaders in Jerusalem (chap. 22, 23); before Felix, Festus, and Herod Agrippa II in Caesarea (chap. 24–26); and finally is taken to Rome, amid many harrowing experiences, including shipwreck (chap. 27, 28). Here, in his own rented house, though constantly chained to a guard,

Paul is free to carry on his preaching and teaching. No wonder "they of Caesar's household" heard and received the Good News of salvation.

Relationship of Acts to the Gospels and the Epistles

Before closing this study, the character of Acts as a central book in the New Testament should be noted. It is the bridge between the Gospels and the Epistles and therefore has close ties to each of these writings.

First, it continues and, in one sense, completes the narrative begun in the Gospels. The earthly life of Christ is followed by the ministry of His apostles.

Second, it shows the fulfillment of our Lord's prophecy of the Church (Matt. 16:18) and prepares the way for the expounding of this subject in the Epistles. Many questions are answered regarding the circumstances of the Church's beginning, early leaders, and growth into a universal fellowship.

Third, Acts gives the background for several of Paul's epistles, relating the details concerning the founding of the churches to which the letters were subsequently written.

Galatians—Antioch, Iconium, Lystra, and Derbe (Acts 13:14–14:28)

Philippians—Philippi (Acts 16:11-40)

1 and 2 Thessalonians—Thessalonica (Acts 17:1-9)

1 and 2 Corinthians—Corinth (Acts 18:1-16)

Ephesians—Ephesus (Acts 19:1-41; 20:17-35; cf. also 1 and 2 Timothy)

By reading these chapters before reading the respective epistles, light is cast on the nature of the city, the people, and the problems faced by Paul.

Fourth, the book of Acts illustrates in the active life of the church many of the principles enunciated in the Epistles. Such matters as organization, discipline, witnessing, evangelism, and teaching are clearly mirrored in the narratives of Acts. Especially prominent is the stress upon the necessity of the work of the Holy Spirit. The early church not only taught this truth but experienced it as well.

DISCUSSION QUESTIONS

1. List Luke's four motives for writing Acts. Show how each is reflected within the narrative.
2. What is the key verse of Acts? In what ways does it provide the framework for the rest of the book?

3. Summarize in your own words the account of the proclamation of the Gospel in Jerusalem (Acts 1:12–8:3).

4. Summarize in your words the account of the proclamation of the Gospel in Judea and Samaria (Acts 8:4–11:18).

5. In what provinces were each of Paul's three missionary journeys centered?

6. Name the two most prominent individuals associated with Paul in each of the three missionary journeys.

7. What is the relationship of the book of Acts to the Gospels and the Epistles?

APPLICATION ACTIVITIES

1. List some of the problems of the early church. How were these solved? Relate these to the present-day church.

2. Appraise the various ministries or some of the outstanding personalities in the book of Acts—especially Stephen, Peter, Philip, and Paul. Observe the influence of the Holy Spirit in each man's life. Compare your observations with your study of the various aspects of Christ's life.

3. List ways that your church can enrich and expand its ministry in various fields of Christian activity. Use the book of Acts as your guide book.

4. For better appreciation of New Testament faith and practice, prepare your own comprehensive outline of the book of Acts.

PAULINE EPISTLES

1 and 2 Thessalonians

As a letter writer and as a man, Paul has no superior in the history of the Church. His life story is one of the most amazing in the history of mankind, and people of all ages since the beginning of the Christian era have, in one way or another, been indebted to him. Before giving attention to the written legacy he has left, the main details of his life must be considered.

The best insights into Paul's life come from his own pen and are to be found in several of the Epistles, particularly Philippians, Galatians, and the Corinthian letters. In addition, the three accounts of Paul's conversion experience and the record of his activities and witness recorded in the book of Acts give valuable information.

BACKGROUND OF PAUL

Paul was first and foremost a Jew. This is the main factor in understanding his character and activities. He was born of Jewish parentage in the city of Tarsus, in the province of Cilicia, and was thus known for many years as Saul of Tarsus. According to his own testimony he was a Pharisee, as his father had been before him (Acts 23:6); he spoke the Aramaic tongue ("a Hebrew of the Hebrews"); and he was taught the trade of tentmaking in his youth (Acts 18:3). Further, Paul was of the tribe of Benjamin (Phil. 3:5). Historically, the Benjamites were fighters, and Paul seems to give evidence of an abundance of zeal in all his endeavors, especially in the persecution of the Church (Gal. 1:13). At an early age he went to Jerusalem, and according to his recorded testimony in Acts, studied under the noted Rabban Gamaliel I, a leading teacher of the School of Hillel (22:3).[1] From Paul's own words in Galatians, we learn that he had "profited in the Jews' religion" beyond many of his fellows, "being more exceedingly zealous of the traditions of my fathers" (1:14).

The beginning of Saul's furious campaign to exterminate the Church coincided with the murder of Stephen (Acts 7:58–8:3). Not only did he persecute "both men and women" in Jerusalem, but, with letters of arrest from the high priest (Joseph Caiaphas), he went to other cities as well to carry on his work (Acts 26:10, 11). It was on one such mission that Saul of Tarsus met Jesus and was dramatically converted.

Saul was a Greek by culture. Not only was he reared in one of the leading centers of Greek learning, but he shows an acquaintance with the Greek mind. As an intelligent scholar, Saul knew many of the commonly used sayings taken from classical and contemporary writers (Acts 17:28; Titus 1:12). He also had a world outlook. Unlike the man of provincial demeanor, Paul could write, "I am made all things to all *men*, that I may by all means save some" (1 Cor. 9:22). Thus, by his background, he was suited to stand before the Gentiles proclaiming Jesus' name.

Further, Saul was a Roman citizen. When questioned about his status by the Roman captain in Jerusalem who had informed his prisoner that he had purchased the coveted citizenship with "a great sum," Paul replied with pride, "But I was actually born *a citizen*" (Acts 22:28 NASB). He had appealed to his citizenship rights earlier in Philippi to gain proper respect from the local magistrates (Acts 16:37-39). This status allowed a number of valuable rights such as the right to a proper trial before condemnation and punishment, the right to appeal to Caesar for justice (cf. Acts 25:11, 12) and, in event of the death penalty, execution by decapitation rather than crucifixion.

CONVERSION OF PAUL

One day it happened! The thing that Saul could never have imagined would happen to him occurred with revolutionary effects. He had denied the Christian claim that Jesus was the Messiah, the Son of God. Further, he did not believe that Christ had risen from the dead as Stephen had proclaimed when he cried, "Behold, I see the heavens opened, and the Son of man standing on the right hand of God" (Acts 7:56). "Liar!" the mob cried and stoned him. Saul stood by "consenting unto his death." But when the Lord Jesus spoke to Saul on the day of the great experience outside Damascus, Saul knew that Stephen had been right and he had been wrong. Jesus was alive after all! And further, He must be the Son of God. Thus, in the synagogues of Damascus, Saul proclaimed Christ as Savior.

To explain exactly what happened to Saul is difficult. But there can be little doubt, from Paul's own testimony, that the change in his life was due to a personal encounter with Christ and a new relationship to Him

(Gal. 2:20; Phil. 3:7ff.; 2 Cor. 5:14-19). While the experience was sudden and dramatic, the effects were enduring. The impact must have necessitated great psychological and intellectual readjustments. This may well account for the period spent in Arabia and Damascus before his first visit to Jerusalem (Gal. 1:16-19). Then he went back to his home territory, and for a period of eight to ten years little is known of his activities.[2]

Paul leaves us in no doubt, however, that Christ had both appointed him an apostle and revealed the Gospel to him, so that he "might preach him among the heathen" (see especially Gal. 1:1-20).

MINISTRY OF PAUL

Paul's missionary labors begin with the invitation of Barnabas to join Paul at Syrian Antioch. For the next twenty years or so Paul carried on a vast ministry.

Background

Beginning in Antioch (Acts 11:25, 26) Paul later evangelized the provinces of Galatia, Macedonia, Achaia, and Asia, besides many smaller areas as well. He founded, established, and organized churches in all these areas.

Together with Barnabas, Peter, James, and other leaders of the Church, Paul had a major part in resolving the problem of the basis of Gentile salvation and the matters of fellowship between Jew and Gentile (cf. Acts 15:1-35; Gal. 2:1-10). Paul's wide outlook and genuine concern that the Gospel might reach out to all the world triumphed over the narrower perspective and more limited concern of the Jerusalem apostles. He had truly caught the vision of his Lord that the message should go out to all nations.

His Written Ministry

At least thirteen samples of Paul's correspondence have been preserved, and he doubtless wrote many others that did not survive.[3] His written ministry shows great diversity, and yet the letters may be naturally grouped under four basic headings, each reflecting a common emphasis. An attempt is also made to indicate an approximate chronological sequence, though any sense of finality here is impossible.

The Eschatological Letters: 1 and 2 Thessalonians (date: about A.D. 50-51)—These epistles emphasize the doctrine of the last things and are especially concerned with the Second Coming of Christ and the implications of that event in the present life of the believer.

The Soteriological Letters: 1 and 2 Corinthians, Galatians, and Romans (date: about A.D. 55-58)[4]—Various aspects of the doctrine of salvation are delineated in this class of letters. The Corinthian Epistles stress the application of salvation to the life of the Church; Romans and Galatians discuss the doctrine of justification and its outward expression in Christian living.

The Christological Letters: Colossians, Philemon, Ephesians, and Philippians (date: about A.D. 60-62)—Often called the Prison Epistles, as they were written (according to tradition as well as internal evidences) from Paul's prison in Rome (Acts 28:30, 31), these letters present the doctrine of Christ in a distinct manner. They contain great passages that highlight the person and work of Christ in a definitive fashion (Col. 1:14-22; 2:3, 9-15; Philem. 15-20; Eph. 1:7-12; Phil. 2:5-11).

The Ecclesiological Letters: 1 Timothy, Titus, and 2 Timothy (date: about A.D. 63-67)—The doctrine of the (local) church is the main theme of these last three letters of Paul, often called the Pastoral Epistles. They deal primarily with the responsibilities of the leaders of the churches. The letters contain detailed instructions regarding the officers, administration, and activities of the church. The last days of Paul are reflected in the closing chapter of 2 Timothy.

1 THESSALONIANS

On his second missionary journey, Paul arrived in Thessalonica, the capital of Macedonia (Acts 17:1-9). Things went well for the missionaries (Silas and Timothy were Paul's companions at this point) until jealous Jews raised a cry against them, charging them with acts "contrary to the decrees of Caesar, saying that there is another king, *one* Jesus" (17:7). Thus they were driven from the city. When Paul arrived later in Corinth (Acts 18), he wrote the letters to the troubled Thessalonican Christians, who had themselves become the objects of persecution since Paul's departure (1 Thess. 2:14). In lieu of a personal visit (1 Thess. 2:17, 18), the apostle expresses his thanks to God for the news brought by Timothy of the firm stand of the believers (1 Thess. 3:6-10).

Outline

Salutation	1:1
Thanksgiving	1:2-10
The Pauline ministry defended	2:1–3:13
The Christian walk delineated	4:1–5:24
Conclusion	5:25-28

Purpose and Content

The Thessalonian Epistles are the only letters of Paul that do not contain an official title of the writer, simply his name (and Silvanus and Timothy) at the beginning. He writes, it would seem, as a personal friend and spiritual adviser to his spiritual children who find themselves beset by afflictions and tribulations. They are perplexed as to why such things should happen to them. Does God care? To encourage them Paul reminds them how he himself was shamefully treated when he came into their city (2:1, 2), and that he had "told you before that we should suffer tribulation" (3:4). All such things are part of the purpose of God.

Since the apostle had departed, some of their number had died. What was to be their attitude toward death? Pagan religion from which they had turned (1:9) held little hope for the afterlife; rather, it was a place of darkness and fear. Would they ever see their loved ones again? On the authority of "the word of the Lord" (4:15), Paul assures them that the dead and living saints shall be one day reunited and "caught up together . . . in the clouds, to meet the Lord in the air" (4:17). This was a word of comfort, indeed. But, on the other hand, the Second Advent called for vigilance as well (5:6). Here is the application of the doctrine to the everyday life of the Christian.

In this letter Paul closes every chapter with some teaching regarding the return of the Lord. In 1:10, the believer is "to wait for [God's] Son from heaven." Paul reminds his readers that they will be his "glory and joy" at the coming of the Lord (2:19, 20). In 3:13, it is the desire of the apostle that the Christians be established "unblameable in holiness before God, even our Father, at the coming of our Lord Jesus Christ with all his saints." A major section follows in 4:13-18, where Paul informs his readers of the reunion of the dead and living saints at the descent of the Lord from heaven, and the entrance into eternal bliss with Him. Finally, 5:23 pictures the believer "preserved blameless unto the coming of our Lord Jesus Christ."[5]

2 THESSALONIANS

Outline

Purpose and Content

Between the time of the writing of the two letters, a new problem had arisen. Apparently someone had caused concern on the part of the believers with regard to their relation to "the Day of the Lord." Paul wrote that they "be not soon shaken in mind, or be troubled, neither by spirit, nor by word, nor by letter as from us, as that the day of Christ is at hand" (2:2).

Why was it that the idea of "the Day of the Lord" should disrupt their peace of mind? Probably because the aspect of this event most prominent in their thinking was that of tribulation, judgment, and destruction. Such a portrayal occurs in many of the related Old Testament passages from which the concept comes (Joel 1:15–2:11; Obad. 15, 16; Zeph. 1:14-18; Zech.14:1-8). It was to be a time that would strike terror into the hearts of men. The Thessalonians had begun to wonder whether they also might fall victim to the Day of Judgment.

It would not be proper to say that there is a simple solution to such a complex problem. The chronological relationships of eschatological events is not always made clear. To be more precise, would these believers find themselves caught in the precarious days of "the great tribulation" that was to come upon the earth? Or, would the Lord take them away before the judgment dawned?

First, Paul said there are certain things which must occur before the full force of God's eschatological judgment will be manifested. There will be apostasy from true religion (2:3); there will be the appearance of the "man of sin" (2:3); and, finally, there will be the removal of a present restrainer (2:6, 7). These will be definite indications of the approaching day of reckoning.

Second, the believers are to be awake and aware of conditions about them and strengthen themselves in their faith (1 Thess. 5:4-8; 2 Thess. 2:15). Thus they will be fortified for any crisis.

Third, and most vital of all, Paul assures the Christians that God is in control. He is working out His purpose, and they are kept within His hand (1 Thess. 5:9, 10, 23, 24; 2 Thess. 1:11, 12; 2:13, 14). This is the ultimate assurance the believer has. The Second Advent not only brings judgment, but blessing also. The prophets had spoken of this aspect with regard to Israel (Joel 2:28-32; Mic. 4:1-5; Zeph. 3:9-20; Mal. 4:2, 3). Paul now informs his readers that they will be with the Lord and share in His victory over His enemies (1:7-10).

Again, as in the first letter, the apostle closes with a number of practical exhortations, especially dealing with the need for honest toil among the Christians. Some of them, thinking that the Lord was to come at once, had ceased working and were becoming a drag upon the rest of the community. An almost certain solution to that problem is given by Paul in 3:10, as he says, "If any would not work, neither should he eat." This is at once a good combination of Christian teaching and common sense. All are to work together while they wait together for the great day of Christ's appearing.

DISCUSSION QUESTIONS

1. What three national cultures affected Paul's life?
2. Show the influence of these varied backgrounds upon Paul's life and ministry.
3. How did Paul's conversion affect his life and teaching?
4. Name four basic categories into which Paul's writings fall and name the books in each.
5. State the doctrine primarily emphasized in each category.
6. What was Paul's experience in Thessalonica on his second missionary journey (Acts 17:1-9)?
7. Name two major problems dealt with by Paul in 1 Thessalonians.
8. With what subject does each chapter of the first epistle close?
9. What doctrinal problem, which arose among believers between the writing of the two Thessalonian Epistles, influenced the content of the second epistle?

APPLICATION ACTIVITIES

1. To assist you in mastering the basic content of the Thessalonian letters, prepare your own outline of these two books.
2. List the passages in Thessalonians relating to Christ's Second Coming in the chronological order of events.
3. With the aid of a topical index, examine other Scripture portions to determine the manner of Christ's Second Coming.
4. List several qualities that are admirable about Paul's life, indicating which impress you most.
5. What features of Paul's conversion are characteristic of all conversions? In what ways was his conversion unique?
6. To assist you in deepening your dedication to the lordship of Christ, list specific ways and means to live in light of His coming. Use the Thessalonian Epistles as a basis for your list.

6

PAULINE EPISTLES

1 and 2 Corinthians

According to the previous classification of Paul's Epistles, these letters are to be considered primarily soteriological, since they deal largely with the subject of salvation. Together with Galatians and Romans, they form the heart of the Pauline writings. Even the radical critics, who have often rejected many of Paul's writings as authentic works, usually have accepted these letters as genuine. The core of Paul's preaching—faith in Christ and dedication to Him—is written large in all of them. His favorite expression, "in Christ," describing the new relationship of the regenerated individual to his Savior and Lord, occurs again and again.

This correspondence emerges from the third missionary journey of Paul (cf. Acts 18:23–21:14). First Corinthians was written from Ephesus (1 Cor. 16:7-9), while 2 Corinthians likely came from Macedonia (see 2 Cor. 2:12, 13; 7:5-7).

1 CORINTHIANS

Background

Paul first visited Corinth on his second journey (Acts 18:1-17). While waiting for Silas and Timothy to come from Macedonia and rejoin him in Corinth, Paul met Aquila and Priscilla and, finding them to be tent-makers as he was, lived with them while carrying on his preaching.

Upon the arrival of his companions, carrying with them news of conditions to the north (in Thessalonica and Berea), Paul reemphasized his proclamation "that Jesus was the Christ" (i.e., Messiah). This brought about the usual reaction from the Jews, and Paul henceforth concentrated on the Gentile ministry in Corinth (Acts 18:6). Before long a number of people became Christians, even including Crispus the ruler of the synagogue. For a period of at least eighteen months Paul continued a systematic teaching program among them.

The event that apparently led to the departure of the apostle from the city was his appearance before Gallio, the proconsul of Achaia, whose residence was in Corinth. As Gallio listened to the arguments of Paul's Jewish accusers, he manifested a calm indifference. This was because it concerned matters of Jewish law, not Roman law, and his courtroom was not the place for religious disputes. It should be said that Gallio's indifference was in reality a blessing, for it diverted the actions of the Jews and set Paul free to continue his work.

While in Ephesus on his third journey (Acts 19:1-41), some of the household of Chloe brought tidings to Paul that things were not well in Corinth (1 Cor. 1:11). In addition, a letter had been sent by the Corinthian church containing a number of problems to which they wished answers from the apostle (1 Cor. 7:1; 8:1; 12:1; 15:12; 16:1). To reply to these and related matters, Paul wrote this first epistle.

Outline

Introduction	1:1-9
Reply to reports from Chloe	1:10–6:20
Reply to the letter from Corinth	7:1–16:9
Conclusion	16:10-24

Purpose and Content

The central concept of the letter is that redemption must be applied to everyday situations. The believer is to remember that the new life in Christ calls for a new way of living. The appeal being made is to the relationship of the Holy Spirit to the believer (3:16, 17; 6:11, 19, 20).

It will help to emphasize these commands if one recalls the character of the city of Corinth. In the first century it was noted for its wickedness and immorality, highlighted by the corrupt, sensual worship of Aphrodite, the Greek goddess of love. Her temple, including a thousand religious prostitutes, stood in manifest contrast to the believer as "the temple of the Holy Spirit" and His demand for righteousness.

In the first section of the letter (chap. 1-6), most of Paul's teaching deals with the problem of authority in the church. The Corinthian believers had been divided by various religious loyalties. Some had appealed to Paul, the leading exponent of the doctrine of justification by faith and of the liberty of the Christian from the bondage of law and the founder of this church. Others sided with Apollos, the learned teacher from Alexandria, filled with the knowledge of the Scriptures. He had followed Paul in his visit to Corinth (Acts 18:24–19:1). There were still others who held that Peter, one of the original disciples of the Lord, with his great love for Christ and his studied concern for the principles of the law of the Lord, was a worthy leader. And finally, there were those who looked with pious disapproval at such discord and exclaimed, "We simply follow Christ!" These last were indeed the worst of all, for they set themselves up above their brethren and sought to keep Christ all to themselves. Paul's crisp answer to all such disputes is given in 3:1-9. Along with his answer Paul calls upon them to gain true spiritual insight and to remember that they are responsible to God—both in the present and one day at the judgment seat (2:1-16; 3:10-23).

Paul dealt with two other matters, sexual immorality (5:1-13; 6:12-20) and lawsuits (6:1-11) in this section. In addition, he rebuked the church for not handling these matters themselves. The former is dealt with by a severe judgment that resulted in the eventual reclaiming of the offender (5:3-5). The latter problem should be cared for, taught Paul, by the church, not in heathen courts. Lawsuits, in fact, are in themselves "a fault among you" (6:7). The final appeal is to maintain the unity and purity of the body of Christ.

In the second section of the letter (chap. 7-16), a number of varied problems appear. The majority of the content, however, relates to the matter of spiritual relationships, either of believers to one another (chap. 7-10) or to situations within the ministries of the church (chap. 11-14). When dealing with the problems of marital relationships, Paul commands that the sanctity of marriage is to be maintained by those contemplating marriage, in the case of a divided household, and by unmarried women. A spiritual basis is in evidence throughout the discussion.

When the problems of conscience are being faced, Paul sets forth a number of guiding principles.[1] First, nothing is permitted to remain in one's life if it causes another Christian to stumble (8:9, 13). Second, the preaching of the Gospel is not to be hindered, rather aided (9:12, 22). Third, all things are to be done "to the glory of God" (10:31).

The ministry of women in the church and the proper conditions for observing the Lord's Supper are discussed in chapter 11. The nature and use of spiritual gifts is the burden of Paul in chapters 12-14. These gifts are to be exercised in love (chap. 13), and all things are to "be done decently and in order" (14:40). This is necessary because all believers are members of one body (12:12-30). Therefore, if the unity of the body is to be maintained, and if the work is to go forward, proper use of spiritual gifts is required.

Only in chapter 15 is a purely doctrinal issue discussed. This is the classic passage in the New Testament on the subject of the resurrection of the body. First, Christ's resurrection is described (v. 1-19). Then, Paul applies this great truth (v. 20-58). Because Christ came out of the grave, so shall all men in God's own time (v. 22). Paul describes the resurrection of the body. It shall be "a spiritual body" (v. 44), that is, characterized by spiritual rather than natural life. Even as our Lord's resurrected body, however, it will be a recognizable form. The great hope of the believer's resurrection is described in verses 50-58 (cf. 1 Thess. 4:13-18).

In closing this lengthy epistle, Paul reminds the Corinthians, as he has done in the Galatian churches, of the collection he is receiving for the needy saints in Jerusalem. That which they give is to be given regularly, voluntarily, and proportionately (16:1, 2).

2 CORINTHIANS

Purpose
One of the most personal of Paul's letters, 2 Corinthians is, for the most part, a defense of Paul's ministry (chap. 1-7) and his apostleship (chap. 10-13). Chapters 8 and 9 consist of an added plea to fulfill their ministry of giving and a pointed reminder that they have been somewhat negligent in the fulfillment of their stewardship.

Outline

Salutation	1:1, 2
Problems of the Christian ministry	1:3–7:16
Problems of Christian giving	8:1–9:15
Problems of a Christian minister	10:1–13:10
Conclusion	13:11-14

Background
After having sent the first epistle to the Corinthian church, Paul waited at Ephesus for their response. He then went north to Troas to meet Titus, but when Titus did not appear Paul continued into Macedonia (2:12, 13). When the two did meet, Paul wrote concerning the Corinthian church that he was comforted by the report of "your earnest desire, your mourning, your fervent mind toward me" (7:7). The news, however, was not all favorable. A vocal element in the church was protesting against the authority of the apostle. Apparently a group of Jewish opponents (11:2) were discounting the reality of Paul's faith in Christ and the genuineness of his ministry (10:2) and were despising his person (10:10). While there had been repentance on the part of some in the church (2:1-11), the unrepentant group continued to press hard upon Paul. Thus Paul bares his inmost feelings here in a way not seen in any other existing letter that he wrote.

Characteristic Features

Amid the multitude of personal references, Paul has given to the church in this letter many enduring doctrinal affirmations. Notice especially the leading references to the character and workings of God (1:3, 4; 2:14; 4:5, 6; 5:18-21; 6:14-18; 9:7-15), the contrast between the old and new covenants (chap. 3), the future state (5:1-10), the ministry of reconciliation (5:14-21), and Christian stewardship of money (chap. 8, 9).

DISCUSSION QUESTIONS

1. Illustrate from these Corinthian Epistles the reasons it may be said that they form the heart of the Pauline writings.
2. Briefly summarize Paul's experiences in Corinth prior to writing 1 Corinthians.
3. What was the immediate occasion for Paul's writing 1 Corinthians?
4. What is the central concept of 1 Corinthians and how can it be fulfilled?
5. Illustrate from Paul's dealing with any three problems in the Corinthian church how Paul's solutions are applicable today.
6. Summarize the teaching of 1 Corinthians 15 concerning the resurrection.
7. What was Paul's major purpose in writing 2 Corinthians?
8. Briefly summarize the background of 2 Corinthians.
9. List several important doctrinal emphases in 2 Corinthians.

APPLICATION ACTIVITIES

1. Select a number of passages that might serve as maxims for a day (e.g., We are ambassadors for Christ). Some find spiritual help from listing a Scriptural maxim at the top of each day's "to do" list.
2. Prepare a list with Scripture references of key doctrinal truths found in the Corinthian Epistles.
3. Discuss to what extent the ways Paul defended himself in 2 Corinthians 10-13 are applicable today.
4. List your significant roles in family and church life (i.e., husband, father, son, church member, and other). Under these headings list Scriptures from the Corinthian Epistles that state guiding principles for these specific roles.

PAULINE EPISTLES

Galatians and Romans

These books emphasize the salvation found in the Corinthian Epistles. Galatians is a sturdy defense of the doctrine that "a man is not justified by the works of the law but by the faith of Jesus Christ" (2:16). In no other writing has Paul so forcibly established the genuineness of his apostolic commission and his message.

GALATIANS

Background

The questions of the date and destination of this letter, as well as the place of writing, are difficult to answer with any certainty. It may well have been the earliest of Paul's writings, penned soon after his first missionary journey upon his return to Syrian Antioch. Thus, it would be dated about A.D. 48/49. But the Epistle has also been placed later by some (as late as A.D. 58, Lightfoot). Even the late date, of course, would still presuppose the lapse of a relatively short period of time after the founding of the Galatian churches.

While the letter is addressed to the churches of Galatia, the matter of destination is problematic due to the first-century meaning of the name itself. That is, "Galatia" could be understood in more than one way. This territory, located in eastern Asia Minor, was settled by the Gauls in the third century B.C. and took its name from these invaders. Eventually, after the Romans came into control of the area, the territory was enlarged. An area to the south was included with the northern section, and the whole new province was called Galatia. When Paul wrote the letter, then, was he addressing people in North Galatia or South Galatia? Most of the older commentators favor the former view; the majority of recent writers favor the latter view. Whichever is accepted, the message of Galatians remains unaffected.

Outline

In examining the structure of the book, one may discern logical steps in Paul's argument. Once he has set the stage for what he has to say (1:1-10), he immediately plunges in to defend his position—that justification before God comes by faith and not by works and that Christ has set us free from the bondage of the law.

Introduction	1:1-10
The autobiographical argument—The Gospel revealed	1:11–2:21
Direct revelation of the Gospel	1:11-24
Apostolic confirmation of the Gospel	2:1-10
Personal application of the Gospel	2:11-21
The doctrinal argument—The Gospel prophesied	3:1–4:31
The personal appeal	3:1-5
The experience of Abraham	3:6-14
The promise and the Law	3:15-22
The nature of sonship	3:23–4:7
The danger of defection	4:8-20
The lesson by allegory	4:21-31
The practical argument—The Gospel applied	5:1–6:10
Conclusion	6:11-18

Purpose and Content

One cannot help but observe that there is no familiar and friendly introduction to this letter as is common in Paul's Epistles. Paul states his business and gets into the details of the argument at once. Paul is amazed that these Christian congregations are wavering so soon in their loyalty to Christ and himself. He roundly condemns those who "pervert the gospel of Christ" (1:6, 7) and calls down the curse of God upon them (1:8, 9).

First, Paul himself has received his Gospel from Christ (1:11, 12). It has not been communicated to him by others; they have only concurred with him in his message and ministry (1:16–2:10). Therefore, on the basis of his own well established experience, he claims that his message is genuine.[1]

Second, the Gospel is not a new thing; it was taught in the Old Testament (3:8). Abraham is the great example of justification by faith in God. As he came into this relationship long before the Law was given, the Law did not justify him—neither can it justify anyone (3:9-14). Paul elaborates this principle by contrasting the "child" with the "son" (3:23–4:7) and drawing upon the story of Abraham's two sons to teach the same truth allegorically (4:21-31).

Third, the Gospel works in personal experience (5:1). When applied, the Gospel gives the individual freedom from bondage to sin, victory over the flesh (the old nature within), and the ability to show forth works of righteousness. All this is set within the framework of the work of the Holy Spirit in the believer's life. "If we live by the Spirit, let us also walk in the Spirit" (5:25).

Thus, in Galatians, probably the earliest of Paul's writings, appears a powerful presentation of the nature of justification. The response of faith on the part of the sinner not only brings him right standing with God, but brings into his life the dynamic of the Spirit to do the work of God.

ROMANS

At the center of "the good tidings of great joy" that were spoken to the shepherds of Bethlehem was a Savior, One who would redeem His people. This subject of redemption is defined and developed by Paul in his letter to the Romans, the most orderly and detailed treatment of salvation in the New Testament.

Background

For many years the apostle had wanted to visit the Christians in Rome (15:23), desiring to establish them in the faith (1:11). While Paul had been heretofore hindered, he stood ready "to preach the gospel to you that are at Rome also" (1:13-15). On his third missionary journey, shortly before leaving Corinth (Acts 20:1-3), Paul wrote this letter in lieu of a visit, and sent it, apparently, by the hand of Phoebe of Cenchrae (16:1, 2). Soon afterward he was arrested in Jerusalem (Acts 21:27ff.). Thus, as it turned out, he did arrive in Rome, but not as a free man (Acts 28:16).

Outline

The theme of the letter is redemption (3:24). Throughout the book Paul carefully develops five aspects of the subject of redemption.

Introduction	1:1-17
Sin—The need for redemption	1:18–3:20
Gentile sin	1:18–2:16
Jewish sin	2:17–3:8
Universal sin	3:9-20
Justification—The provision of redemption	3:21–5:21
Sanctification—The effect of redemption	6:1–8:39
The union with Christ	6:1-23
The conflict of natures	7:1-25
The victory by the Spirit	8:1-39

Purpose and Content

Paul's introductory words combine many remarks of a personal and a theological nature (1:1-17). He tells a good deal about himself. He is a bondservant of Christ, yet an apostle (1:1). His commission is to the nations (1:5). He is a man of prayer (1:9, 10), an earnest worker (1:13-15), and unashamed of the message he proclaims (1:16). Along with this, he describes the Gospel as being prophesied in the Old Testament (1:2), centered in the Son of God (1:3), "dynamite" that brings salvation to those who believe it (1:16), and a revelation of God's righteousness to the faithful ones (1:17).

The first major division of the epistle (1:18–3:20) delineates the sinful condition of man and demonstrates the universal need for redemption. Common to the descriptions of various classes of persons is a picture of spiritual and moral degeneration. Indeed, the former leads to the latter.

Man has turned away from God and fallen into idolatry (1:21-23); thus "God gave them up" (1:24, 26, 28). Some have condemned their fellowmen, but they are in reality worthy of condemnation themselves (2:1-3), for they practice the same things. God "will render to every man according to his deeds" (2:6). Gentiles, without the written law of the Jews, have the voice of conscience within (2:14, 15). With all his privileges, the Jew himself has not maintained his spiritual life, and the name of God is blasphemed among the Gentiles because of Jewish failure (2:24, 25). The final verdict declares the guilt of all before the righteousness of God. By works "shall no flesh be justified in his sight" (3:20).

Then the provision of God is declared (3:21–5:21). Justification is the answer—and it is "by faith of Jesus Christ unto all and upon all them that believe" (3:22). God is able to maintain His own righteousness and yet declare the sinner righteous because of the redeeming work of Christ (3:24-26). To illustrate the principle of justification by faith, Paul draws upon the example of Abraham (as he had done earlier in Galatians), showing that Abraham's acceptance preceded both the institution of circumcision and the giving of the Law; thus it was by his faith alone that he was declared righteous (4:10-13). Having been justified, the sinner is able to realize some of the benefits (5:1-11) that accrue from the work of the Lord Jesus (5:12-21).

Next, the logical effect of redemption is discussed (6:1–8:39). The implications of the new relationship with God are far-reaching. A new life (6:11) and a new loyalty (6:12-14) should be manifested. Despite the constant demands of the old nature to dominate (7:24), there is victory through the work of the Holy Spirit (chap. 8). He empowers (8:16) and intercedes (8:26). Surely the Lord's promise is true, "My grace is sufficient for thee" (2 Cor. 12:9).

Following this, Paul makes clear the universal nature of the message (9:1–11:36). It is to both Jew and Gentile. Though God may have set aside His people Israel, He has not cast them off (11:1). He is sovereign and is only working out His purpose of redemption (9:19-32). There is yet a day of restoration and blessing for Israel (11:25-32). In the present day, the Gospel goes out to all and "whosoever shall call upon the name of the Lord shall be saved" (10:13).

In the last major division of the letter, Paul describes the outworking of redemption (12:1–15:13). Beginning with a plea for complete dedication to the Lord (12:1, 2),[2] Paul goes on to show the varied responsibilities and relationships of the Christian. The Christian is to evaluate himself sanely in the light of the grace of God; to fulfill his ministry within the church (12:3-8); and to have proper relationships to other individuals (12:9-21), to government (13:1-7), to society (13:8-14), and to Christians who differ from him in personal scruples (14:1–15:13).

The concluding words are largely personal in nature, consisting of the hopes and plans of the apostle, especially with reference to Paul's visit to Rome, and a list of greetings to friends and fellow workers in the church (15:14–16:27).

DISCUSSION QUESTIONS

1. What significant doctrine does Galatians clearly defend?
2. State the basic claims presented by Paul in Galatians as to the genuineness of his message.
3. What was the occasion of Paul's writing the Epistle to the Romans?
4. What Old Testament character does Paul use in Romans and Galatians to illustrate justification by faith? What is the significance of the time this character appeared in Old Testament sequence?
5. According to Galatians 5:1-24 and Romans 6-8, how does a Christian live a spiritual life?

6. How can a man be justified by God (Rom. 3:21–5:21)?
7. Referring to the outline and Scripture divisions of the book of Romans, summarize briefly Israel's past, present, and future.
8. State some of the main responsibilities the Christian has in doing the will of God (Romans 12–15).

APPLICATION ACTIVITIES

1. For a better comprehension of Romans and Galatians, expand the outlines given in this text.
2. Utilizing your Bible concordance or index, contrast the use of the words *law* and *grace* or *faith* and *works* in the Bible.
3. In a panel discussion, consider ways in which Christian liberties are sometimes abused, and suggest remedies.
4. Using verses only from the book of Romans, outline the steps leading to salvation.
5. Referring to interpretive news periodicals such as *Newsweek* and *Time*, trace significant developments in contemporary history that appear to be fulfillment of prophecy concerning the Jews. Why should the Christian be alert to these?

PAULINE EPISTLES

Colossians, Philemon, Ephesians, Philippians

A misfortune or a blessing? How is Paul's imprisonment to be viewed? Would it have been better for all concerned if Paul had remained a free man and able to carry on his missionary travels? Or did God direct Paul into such a situation as this? Possibly the question may never be settled to the satisfaction of all, but this point is clear: the period that Paul spent in the Roman prison (Acts 28:30, 31) was one of the richest of his career. It provided him an entrance into the household of the emperor (Phil. 1:13; 4:22) and brought forth the Prison Epistles—the most profound and Christ-exalting examples of Paul's written works.

Each of these letters contains references to Paul's situation. In Colossians 1:24 and 4:18, he speaks of his "sufferings" and his "bonds." Philemon 1, 9, and 10 refer to him as a prisoner and one in bonds. Again, in Ephesians 3:1, 4:1, and 6:20, Paul makes mention of being a prisoner and "in a chain." Finally, Philippians 1:12, 13 calls attention to his bonds and the presence of the whole praetorian guard. Given this evidence, the place of Paul's imprisonment has been traditionally held to have been Rome.

COLOSSIANS

Here is one of two epistles written by Paul to churches he had not personally founded. It seems likely that during his lengthy stay at Ephesus (Acts 19) the message of Christ had been taken to Colossae by one of his fellow workers. He describes Epaphras, a Colossian Christian serving with Paul (4:12), as "our dear fellow servant, who is for you a faithful minister of Christ; who also declared unto us your love in the Spirit" (1:7, 8).

Background

Colossae did not rank with Ephesus in either size or importance. It was an inland city, lying beside the Lycus River, near Laodicea and Hierapolis (cf. 4:13). Located on the main commercial thoroughfare between East and West, the city was influenced by contrasting ideologies. These influences seem to be reflected in the epistle as Paul writes to describe the person of Christ (cf. 1:14-20) and to correct the current errors relating to redemption and the pattern of Christian living (2:8–3:4).

The name usually given to the false teaching in this city is the Colossian heresy. This heresy apparently consisted of a mixture of Jewish and Gnostic ideas, combined to create a threat to the Gospel of Christ. The unsound teaching sought to reduce Christianity to a legal system and to obscure the person and work of Christ. Paul attacks the errors at Colossae by a clear presentation of counter truths. The key verse is 1:18—"that in all *things* he might have the preeminence."

Outline

Salutation	1:1, 2
The prayer of thanksgiving	1:3-8
The prayer of intercession	1:9-4
The supremacy of Christ	1:15-23
Paul's desire for the saints	1:24–2:7
Paul's exhortations to the saints	2:8–4:6
Paul's representatives to Colossae	4:7-9
Greetings	4:10-17
Conclusion	4:18

Comparison with Ephesians

As one reads this epistle, he or she may be impressed with its likeness to Ephesians. Indeed, the two may be called the twin epistles of the New Testament. They are most nearly alike in their presentation of Christ and His body, the Church. In Colossians, Christ is "the head of the body" (1:18); in Ephesians, it is "the church, which is his body" (1:22, 23). The development in Colossians, then, concentrates on the exalted position of Christ; in Ephesians, upon the nature of the Church.

Another notable likeness is the section dealing with the application of the Gospel to practical affairs. Both epistles describe the old man and new man together with the evidences of each (Col. 3:9, 10; Eph. 4:22-24). Also, each contains commands to the various members of the household to fulfill their rightful functions (Col. 3:18–4:1; Eph. 5:22–6:9).

Purpose and Content

The key passages telling of Christ are to be found in 1:15-23 and 2:8–3:4. In the first, Christ is described as preeminent in at least four distinct relationships: to God (1:15); to created things (1:16, 17); to the Church

(1:18); and to the work of redemption (1:19-23). This discussion is preliminary and necessary to expose the heresy described in chapter 2. The presentation of the superiority of Christ is the answer to all such errors. This is Paul's basic approach in the section that follows.

In reading 2:8–3:5, the main characteristics of this false teaching seem to be:

1. Rationalistic philosophy that denied revelation (2:8).

2. Legalistic religion that was seriously endangering the concept of Christian liberty (2:16).

3. Voluntary humility and worship of angels, based on a superior knowledge (2:18).

The responses Paul gives to each of these aspects of false teaching are as follows (in corresponding order):

1. Christ is the fullness of God, and the One in whom the Christian is "made full" (2:9).

2. Christ is the reality, the fulfillment of the types and shadows of ceremonial religion (2:17). In Him, these types are done away.

3. Christ is the Head (2:19). If He is not given His proper place, things will come in that are in reality useless for spiritual life (2:23).

Finally, Paul shows the implications of these teachings. A new kind of life, a new way of living is demanded (3:5-17). The person in whom the Word of Christ "dwells" richly will give evidence of this new life (3:16, 17). Paul emphasizes especially domestic relationships:

Wives—be in subjection to your husbands (3:18)

Husbands—love your wives (3:19)

Children—obey your parents (3:20)

Fathers—do not provoke your children (3:21)

Servants—obey your masters; you really serve Christ (3:22-25)

Masters—treat your servants justly (4:1)

Thus, Christ is not only to be preeminent in one's doctrine, but in his duties as well.

PHILEMON

Background

Along with constituting a part of the New Testament canon, this brief epistle is a prime example of Paul's personal correspondence. It is a letter written by one Christian to another, asking that a favor be granted because of their mutual relationship to Christ and to each other. It is a masterful example of the tactful approach to a delicate and difficult situation. The letter was sent along with the letter to the Colossians to Philemon, in whose house the Colossian church met.

Outline

Salutation	1-3
The prayer for Philemon's ministry	4-7
The petition for Onesimus' restoration	8-21
The prospect of Paul's visit	22
Conclusion	23-25

Purpose

Within the framework of Christology, Paul here illustrates the principle of forgiveness and restoration on the basis of substitution. He asks that Onesimus, the slave who is worthy of punishment, be forgiven by his master and received back "not now as a servant, but above a servant, a brother beloved" (16).

Paul beseeches and offers to pay any debt himself that stands due to Philemon (18, 19). Thus the doctrine of imputation is illustrated. The merit of one person is reckoned to the account of another.[1]

EPHESIANS

Background

Ephesus, in the first century A.D., called herself the first city of Asia. Although the ancient city of Pergamum (cf. Rev. 2:12), just to the north, was still the official capital of the province, Ephesus had risen rapidly in stature. An important center commercially, intellectually, and religiously, she boasted one of the seven wonders of the ancient world: the ornate, glistening temple of Diana, the great goddess of the Ephesians (cf. Acts 19:23ff.).

The history of the Ephesian church may be traced in some detail through the New Testament. Paul founded and established the church as was recorded in Acts 19 and 20. Having received the apostle's teaching for over two years, the church was well grounded in the faith. The Ephesian Epistle reflects the spiritual capacity of this church (notice especially Eph. 1:3-14). Further, the letter warns against the conflict with evil spirits (6:10ff.), which were a menace in this city (cf. Acts 19:11-17).

The letters to Timothy, who was left in Ephesus by Paul to carry on the work (1 Tim. 1:3ff.), show the next stage in the history. False teachers had begun to trouble the believers, and Paul sends instructions regarding sound teaching and the proper organization of the church. In Revelation 2:1-7, the last chapter is written concerning this church in the

New Testament. It is a sad word—she has left her "first love" for Christ (2:4). When she did not repent of her condition, as church history shows, she was removed—her lampstand no longer shone as a witness in Ephesus.

Outline

The central theme of the epistle is the Church as the body of Christ. Paul has given a sublime presentation of this truth from the very inception of the Church to its witness within the world and its conflict against the forces of evil.

Salutation	1:1, 2
The Church in the purpose of God	1:3-14
The Church and the power of God	1:15–2:10
The Church as the household of God	2:11-22
The Church as the revelation of God	3:1-13
The Church and the fullness of God	3:14-21
The Church and the standards of God	4:1–6:9
The Church and the armor of God	6:10-20
Conclusion	6:21-24

Purpose and Content

The letter is addressed to believers, described as "the saints" and "the faithful." One emphasizes the believer's position in Christ, the other his character before God.

In the first part of the epistle (1:3-14) Paul concisely describes the origin of the Church, here in its universal aspect, in the purpose of God. He highlights such important themes as election (1:4), predestination (1:5, 11), adoption (1:5), redemption (1:7), purpose (1:9, 10), and the sealing with the Holy Spirit (1:13), culminating in the final possession of the Church by God (1:14).[2]

By God's power the Church has been called into being (1:15–2:10) and is described as a great household, consisting of both Jew and Gentile (2:11-22), sharing alike in the riches of God's inheritance (3:1-13). God dwells within the Church, which has been built upon a solid foundation and is being made up of many parts, each having its own place in the structure (2:19-22).

The two concepts of "walk" and "warfare" are characteristic of the practical division of the book (4:1–6:24). While the word *walk,* denoting one's manner of life, appears twice in the early chapters (2:2, 10), it is more common in the last part (4:1, 17; 5:2, 8, 15). The Christian is to "walk worthy," "walk not as other Gentiles," "walk in love," "walk as children of light," and "walk circumspectly." He is to walk in keeping with his position as a member of the body of Christ (cf. 1 John 2:5, 6).

The exhortations to the members of the household are generally lengthier than in the Colossian letter. In Ephesians, Paul gives much attention to the wife-husband relationship, using it as an illustration of Christ and the Church (5:32).[3] An abbreviated comparison of the two passages should make apparent the leading features of each:

Ref.	Ephesians	Ref.	Colossians
5:22-24	*Wives:* be subject to your own husbands	3:18	*Wives:* be subject to your husbands
5:25-31	*Husbands:* love your wives; notice Christ's example	3:19	*Husbands:* love your wives; do not be bitter against them
6:1-3	*Children:* obey your parents; it is God's command	3:30	*Children:* obey your parents; this is the right thing to do
6:4	*Fathers:* provoke not your children, but nurture them	3:21	*Fathers:* provoke not your children, lest they be discouraged
6:5-8	*Servants:* be obedient to your masters; serve the Lord	3:22-25	*Servants:* be obedient to your masters; work heartily, as unto the Lord
6:9	*Masters:* serve the Lord; forbear threatening; you have a Master in heaven	4:1	*Masters:* render just and equal dues to your servants; you have a Master in heaven

In closing the Epistle to the Ephesians, the apostle deals with the Christian's warfare (literally, wrestling or hand-to-hand combat) against the spiritual forces of darkness (6:10-20). The Christian's provision against this foe is the whole armor of God. Using it will enable the Christian "to stand against the wiles of the devil" (v. 11).[4] Paul describes the various pieces of the armor and their function.

Thus, while the Christian finds himself "in the heavenly places" (1:3, 10, 20; 2:6; 3:10; 6:12), he is also to avail himself of all God's provisions and give careful heed to all His demands for his life and warfare upon the earth.

PHILIPPIANS

"Rejoice in the Lord always: *and* again I say, Rejoice" (4:4). This note characterizes the Philippian letter. A proper appreciation of Paul's great faith in God makes joy seem a natural expression in spite of adverse circumstances.

Background

The city of Philippi was the starting point for the preaching of the Gospel in Europe. Paul sailed from Troas, following the Macedonian vision (Acts 16:9), "assuredly gathering that the Lord had called us for to preach the gospel unto them" (Acts 16:10). He arrived in a city that had an illustrious history. It was on this site that, in 42 B.C., the famous battle was fought between Octavian and Antony against Brutus and Cassius. Following the battle, the status of a Roman colony was conferred upon the city by the victorious Octavian. Thus it came to be modeled after the imperial city of Rome. The people were proud of their rights of citizenship (Acts 16:20, 21). Through the city ran the famous Via Egnatia, the trade route between East and West.

When Paul, Silas, Timothy, and Luke arrived here, they preached first to a group of women gathered for prayer near the river (Acts 16:13). These, among them Lydia and her family, later constituted the nucleus of the church in the city. Soon, however, trouble arose. When Paul and Silas expelled a demon from a slave girl, her masters seeing their gain from her services was gone (Acts 16:19) had the two imprisoned on a false charge. But an earthquake during the night liberated them from prison, their jailer became a Christian (Acts 16:34), and their appeal to their Roman citizenship freed them from further punishment (cf. Acts 16:22-24, 38-40). Years later, at the time of the writing of this letter, Paul was a prisoner again! This time, due to false accusations also, he had been sent to Rome in chains. Yet he penned an epistle that radiates joy and speaks often of the good tidings, the Gospel of Christ. This is a demonstration of his testimony, "For to me to live *is* Christ" (Phil. 1:21).

Outline

As the epistle is composed of many personal matters, the structure is not as clear-cut as many of Paul's other writings. The underlying theme, however, is the Gospel, and the key words are *joy* and *rejoice*.

Salutation	1:1, 2
Thanksgiving and prayer for the saints	1:3-11
Paul and his circumstances	1:12-26
Believers and their conduct	1:27-30
Christ and His example—Humility	2:1-18
Timothy and Epaphroditus and their concern	2:19-30
Paul and his example—Maturity	3:1–4:1
Exhortations and appreciation	4:2-20
Conclusion	4:21-23

Purpose and Content

Viewing the major features of the letter, one is readily able to see that the chief hortatory sections deal with the concepts of unity through humility (2:1-18) and maturity in Christ (3:1–4:1). A number of specific applications of this maturity are given in 4:2-20.

The main personal sections concern Paul himself (1:12-26; 3:4-14; 4:10-20) and two of his fellow workers, Timothy and Epaphroditus (2:19-30). The leading doctrinal passage concerns the incarnation and exaltation of Christ (2:5-11). In every kind of situation, Christ is exalted: in Paul's own sufferings (1:12-26); in the Christian's personal life (2:1-5); in Paul's own desires and ambitions (3:7-14); and in his realization of true serenity (4:10-18).

By His own example, Christ has shown the way of acceptance with God. The lowly place precedes the exalted position. Though the qualities of deity were resident within Him (2:6), Christ willingly relinquished His prerogatives to accomplish the work of the Cross (2:7, 8). Thus, God exalted Him to the supreme place over every creature; to Him every knee must bow (2:9-11). This is the Christ whom Paul desires to know in daily experience (3:10), and the One whom we await from heaven "Who shall change our vile body . . . like unto his glorious body" (3:20, 21).

DISCUSSION QUESTIONS

1. Why are Colossians, Philemon, Ephesians, and Philippians called Prison Epistles?
2. What was the Colossian heresy?
3. List several reasons for calling Colossians and Ephesians the twin epistles of the New Testament.
4. In the book of Colossians, Paul deals with what major domestic relationships?
5. How is the doctrine of imputation illustrated in the book of Philemon?
6. Briefly trace the history of the Ephesian church as portrayed in the New Testament.
7. What is the central theme of the book of Ephesians?
8. Name at least three of Paul's experiences in Philippi prior to his writing the Philippian Epistle.
9. Why was it possible for Paul to have the major theme that he had in his letter to the Philippians in spite of his experiences?

APPLICATION ACTIVITIES

1. In each of the epistles studied in this chapter, find one or more significant indications of Paul's attitude during the days of his imprisonment.

2. Utilizing key phrases from these four epistles, draw a word portrait of Christ. -OR- Expand the chart you prepared in chapter 1, activity #1.

3. Trace specific scriptural commands and guiding principles that apply directly to your various roles in life. -OR- Expand the chart begun in chapter 6, activity #4.

4. For personal enrichment, trace and summarize the use of the words "in Christ" as found in Ephesians and Colossians.

5. Prepare your own outline for one or more of the epistles covered in this chapter.

9

PAULINE EPISTLES

1 Timothy, Titus, 2 Timothy

The last group of epistles in the Pauline collection have been named the Pastoral Epistles because of their emphasis on the personal responsibilities and the public functions of the pastor (literally, shepherd) of the local church. Written to two of Paul's closest companions, Timothy and Titus, these are the latest of Paul's letters, usually dated near the end of his life, about A.D. 63-67. Especially in 2 Timothy Paul seems to anticipate the end (cf. 4:6).

Although scholars are divided on the matter of the authorship of these books, the three letters are here assumed to be Pauline.[1] They reflect Paul's life between the time of his imprisonment mentioned in Acts and his death some years later.

1 TIMOTHY

Background

Apparently converted under the preaching of Paul on his first mission to Galatia, Timothy enters the pages of the New Testament in Acts 16:1ff. As Paul made a return journey into the same territory, he found Timothy, likely in Lystra. Timothy is called by the apostle "*my* own son in the faith" (1 Tim. 1:2) and "*my* dearly beloved son" (2 Tim.1:2). Having been reared by his mother, a Jewess (although his father was a Greek, Acts 16:1, 3), Timothy knew the Old Testament Scriptures from his childhood (2 Tim. 3:14, 15) and now, being converted to Christianity, was "well reported of by the brethren that were at Lystra and Iconium" (Acts 16:2).

Timothy accompanied Paul from this time onward, being left later in Ephesus to straighten out the affairs of the church, particularly some doctrinal difficulties, and to oversee its organization and deportment (cf. 1 Tim. 1:3ff.; 3:1-14; 4:6-16). When Paul wrote to him from Rome, he asked Timothy to come soon to visit him, bringing John Mark with him and also some personal belongings (2 Tim. 4:9, 11, 13). We do not know whether or not Timothy arrived before Paul's death.

From the contents of these letters, as well as scattered references in other epistles, Timothy may be pictured as a faithful, diligent worker, dear to Paul's heart (cf. Phil. 2:19, 20). The fact that the great apostle entrusted Timothy with the responsibility of a leading church, bears testimony to Paul's confidence in his companion. It may also be concluded that Timothy needed occasional prodding and encouragement by Paul, possibly due to a natural timidity (cf. 2 Tim. 1:6, 7; 1 Tim. 4:12-16). As a "man of God" (1 Tim. 6:11), he was exhorted to emulate his Lord "who before Pontius Pilate witnessed a good confession" (6:13) and to "keep that which is committed to thy trust" (6:20).

Purpose

The letter has a double aspect. One is the emphasis upon Timothy as a person—he has certain responsibilities to fulfill as a minister of the Lord and as an exemplary individual. The other is the emphasis upon his official responsibilities—he is to see that the church is properly taught, organized, and administered. The former aspect is seen particularly in 1:3-7, 18-20; 4:6-16; 5:1ff.; 6:11-21; the latter particularly in chapters 2, 3, 5, and 6:1-10. As might be expected, there is not a hard and fast line between the two. Personal and official responsibilities cannot logically be separated.

Outline

Salutation	1:1, 2
Charge to Timothy	1:3-20
Exhortations for church order—Prayer and worship	2:1-15
Requirements for church officers—Elders and deacons	3:1-13
Parenthesis	3:14-16
Instructions for church activities	4:1–6:21a
Conclusion	6:21b

Basic Features

As more will be said about Timothy himself in the second letter, special attention is given here to the basic features of church organization and administration.

First, the ideal church should be characterized by proper prayer life (chap. 2). Regulations for the objects of prayer are first given (v. 1-4), then for the respective functions of men and women in the church (v. 8-15). Emphasis is upon the proper attitudes in prayer and service, rather than upon outward appearances. Men are assigned the place of official teachers and administrators.

Second, the ideal church should be characterized by proper organization (3:1-13). The requirements for elders, deacons, and the women (deaconesses?) are enumerated in this passage. They relate both to the moral and spiritual qualities of the person desiring an office, and to the functions he is expected to perform. The first-century church held high standards, indeed.

Third, the ideal church should be characterized by proper administration of its various affairs (5:1–6:10). Emphasis is placed here first upon the care for and the responsibilities of widows (5:3-16). If a widow is aged and desolate, let the church care for her. If she has children or grandchildren, let them care for her. If she is a young widow, Paul recommends remarriage and rearing of a family. Following this, instructions are given regarding the work of the elders (5:17-25), the servants (6:1, 2), and the teachers (6:3-10). Each is to discharge his responsibilities knowing that he is answerable to the Lord.

TITUS

Background

Like Timothy, Titus also appears to have been led to Christ by Paul. The apostle calls him "*mine* own son after the common faith" (Titus 1:4). He was a Greek, possibly from Syrian Antioch. When Paul and Barnabas went from Antioch to Jerusalem to discuss their ministry with the leaders of the church there, Titus accompanied them (Gal. 2:1-3). He is presented as an example of a Gentile become Christian without the necessity of Jewish circumcision. Titus thus illustrates the principle of which Paul speaks in Galatians 2:16.

Strange as it may seem, the name of Titus does not appear in the book of Acts. Of all the major companions of the apostle Paul, only Titus and Luke are not mentioned there by name, although Luke is included anonymously in the "we sections."

The chief picture which we gain of Titus, aside from the references in the epistle that bears his name, is found in 2 Corinthians. He seems to have been the kind of person we today call a trouble shooter, thus he was sent by Paul into difficult situations to attempt a solution. Paul rejoices, as he writes to the Corinthians, in that he was comforted by the return of Titus from Corinth because the apostle's hopes for the church seem to have been justified. Apparently Titus had been successful in smoothing the troubled waters (2 Cor. 7:6-10, 13-16). He had been sent to see about the promised contribution for the Jerusalem church. Having been lax in fulfilling this ministry, the Corinthians were urged by Paul to demonstrate to his fellow workers "the proof of your love, and of our boasting on your behalf" (cf. 2 Cor. 8:6, 16, 17, 23, 24).

We see in the Epistle to Titus that Paul had left his companion in the island of Crete to "set in order the things that were wanting, and ordain elders in every city" (1:5). As in the case of Timothy in Ephesus, Titus was given the responsibility of organizing and administering the affairs of these churches, together with carrying on a sound program of teaching. His last appearance in the New Testament is in 2 Timothy 4:10 where he has left Rome and gone to Dalmatia, apparently to represent Paul once again.

The epistle itself has as its theme "sound doctrine" (cf. 1:9; 2:1, 7, 8). Proper understanding of the truth should eventuate in good works (cf. 1:16; 2:7, 14; 3:1, 8, 14). The good works are not the basis of salvation (3:5) but are to be the evidence of it (3:8).

Outline

Salutation	1:1-4
Paul's instructions to Titus	1:5–3:11
Regarding the churches	1:5-16
Regarding individuals	2:1-15
Regarding the world	3:1-8
Regarding heresies	3:9-11
Personal notes	3:12-14
Conclusion	3:15

Purpose and Content

It appears that the chief problem in Crete came from false teachers, mainly "of the circumcision" (i.e., Jewish), who are described by Paul as "unruly and vain talkers and deceivers" (1:10). They were teaching "Jewish fables" (1:14) and introducing "foolish questions, and genealogies, and contentions, and strivings about the law" (3:9). Along with this was the moral laxity of the Cretans (1:12, 13) and the careless demeanor of some of the members of the church (2:2, 3, 10; 3:2). To counteract such vanities, Paul urges upon Titus the need for sound doctrine, emphasizing that the Word of God is the basis for the Christian life (cf. 1:3; 2:5, 10). When this teaching is properly received, good works should result.

The doctrine of God is also prominent in the epistle. Several of the references relate to the Father (1:1, 3, 4; 2:10; 3:4); others to the Son (1:4; 2:13; 3:6); and to the Holy Spirit (3:5).

The doctrine of salvation is central in 2:11-14 and 3:4-7. The grace of God not only saves, but also instructs the believer and gives him the blessed hope. Those who have been redeemed are to show a change in character (v. 14). Notice, too, the four important words describing God's character in relation to salvation: "kindness," "love" (3:4), "mercy" (3:5), and "grace" (3:7).

As compared with 1 Timothy, the instructions regarding church officers are more brief in Titus. Here only the elder (or bishop) is described; the deacons are not mentioned. Once again the need for men of high spiritual and moral qualities is stressed. They must be both exemplary in character and capable in their functions. "In all things shewing thyself a pattern of good works . . . that they may adorn the doctrine of God our Saviour in all things" (2:7a, 10b).

2 TIMOTHY

Background

At the time of the writing of this letter, Paul was awaiting execution. According to tradition, he was imprisoned in the Mamertine dungeon in Rome, under circumstances much less favorable than those of Acts 28:30. He seems to expect death rather than release (4:6; contrast Phil. 1:19; Philem. 22).

Purpose and Content

Thus these are the final recorded words of Paul in the New Testament. With special interest we look into these pages for thoughts of the great apostle as he faces the end of his life and ministry. As he faces death alone, except for the companionship of Luke the physician (4:11), Paul's chief concern is for the welfare of Timothy and the success of his work in Ephesus. The leading exhortations that appear throughout the letter are worthy of careful attention:

"Stir up the gift of God, which is in thee." (1:6)

"Be not thou therefore ashamed . . . but be thou partaker of the afflictions." (1:8)

"Hold fast the form of sound words." (1:13)

"That good thing which was committed unto thee keep by the Holy Ghost." (1:14)

"The things that thou hast heard of me among many witnesses, the same commit thou to faithful men." (2:2)

"Of these things put *them* in remembrance." (2:14)

"Study to shew thyself approved unto God." (2:15)

"Flee also youthful lusts." (2:22)

"Continue thou in the things which thou hast learned." (3:14)

"Preach the word." (4:2)

"Watch thou in all things . . . make full proof of thy ministry." (4:5) These constitute the major thrust of the epistle. It is a letter of personal counsel.

Outline

Salutation	1:1, 2
Thanksgiving for Timothy	1:3-18
Exhortations to Timothy	2:1-26
Warnings to Timothy	3:1-17
The final charge to Timothy	4:1-8
Personal instructions to Timothy	4:9-21
Conclusion	4:22

Characteristic Features

Brief consideration should be given to two or three of the outstanding passages in the epistle. Chapter 2 is characterized by the seven metaphors used to describe the believer. Paul, by the use of these varied figures of speech, makes clear to Timothy the differing facets of the Christian's ministry and the responsibility connected with each.

As a *child,* he is to be strong and active. (v. 1, 2)

As a *soldier,* he is to suffer hardship and also please his superior. (v. 3, 4)

As an *athlete,* he is to obey the rules of the game. (v. 5)

As a *husbandman* (farmer), he is to labor and thus have full participation in the results. (v. 6)

As a *workman,* he is to be diligent, rightly handling the Word of God. (v. 15)

As a *vessel,* he is to be honorable, ready for the Master's use. (v. 21)

As a *servant,* he is to be gentle and helpful. (v. 24, 25)

In 3:14-17, one of the classic passages on the nature of the Scriptures appears. The nature of the Scriptures (the written Word) is divine; they are "inspired of God." God has "breathed them out" to men; the result is His Word communicated faithfully. They are able to (1) enlighten one unto salvation (v. 15) and (2) thoroughly equip the man of God (v. 17).

The letter ends with a series of personal remarks, including the request that Timothy visit Paul soon (4:9), before the winter season if possible (4:21). While in his prison cell Paul wanted his cloak for warmth and his books for study. To the very end of his life Paul remained active and alert. "I have fought a good fight, I have finished my course, I have kept the faith: henceforth there is laid up for me a crown of righteousness, which the Lord, the righteous judge, shall give me at that day" (4:7, 8).

DISCUSSION QUESTIONS

1. Why are these epistles called the Pastoral Epistles? Illustrate your answer with references from the letters.
2. What was Timothy's family and spiritual background prior to his joining Paul in ministry?
3. Describe the characteristics of Timothy as a Christian worker.
4. How did Paul show his confidence in Timothy?
5. What three basic features should characterize the church according to 1 Timothy?
6. In what ways did Titus demonstrate his abilities as a problem solver?
7. What is the theme of the book of Titus?
8. In what ways were false teachers causing problems in Crete?
9. State several of the leading exhortations of Paul to Timothy as found in 2 Timothy.
10. List several of the metaphors Paul uses in 2 Timothy to describe the believer.

APPLICATION ACTIVITIES

1. Compile some maxims for Christians as found in 2 Timothy. -OR- Expand your list of maxims prepared for chapter 6, activity #1.
2. As you see the picture of Paul in 2 Timothy just before his death, what facts impress you most?
3. Prepare a list of standards for church leaders, based on these Pastoral Epistles and applicable for today's situations.
4. Describe the dangers facing the church in Paul's day in present-day terminology and as though affecting your own church.
5. To develop your ability to summarize Bible truths, prepare your own outline for each of these three books.

10

THE CHURCH AND SUFFERING

James, Hebrews, 1 Peter

There were periods during the first century when the church, in one place or another, felt the pangs of suffering and hardship. These trials came from various sources and, to some extent, for different reasons. Nevertheless, they were equally distressing, and the Christians were at times perplexed as to the purpose of all these things in their experience.

If James is rightly dated at about A.D. 45, and thus the earliest book in the New Testament, it reflects trial in the church not long after the time of its inception (Acts 2). It describes trials from without (1:2) and within (1:13-15), recalls suffering as seen in earlier days by the prophets and Job (5:10, 11), and exhorts the suffering person to pray (5:13). The book, apparently meant for Jewish converts of the Dispersion (1:1), is really a treatise on the faith that endures in the face of all types of obstacles.

Hebrews, also written to Jewish converts, makes references to the sufferings of believers. Written at a later date than James (probably shortly before A.D. 70), it is an exhortation to Christians to press forward, to endure, even in the face of serious pressures (cf. 12:3ff.). Whether or not it was written in or near Rome, it reflects the serious conditions existing at that time, near the end of the reign of Nero.

First Peter, to a much greater degree, is also concerned with this problem. The word *suffering* occurs seventeen times, being used both of the sufferings of Christ and His people. The problem is particularly reflected in 4:12-19. By this time (about A.D. 63-65) the pressure of Nero's persecution of the Roman Christians may have been felt in some of the provinces as well (cf. 1:1) or at least the threat was present. Thus, Peter writes to give hope by furnishing a proper perspective (cf. 1:6-9).

JAMES

Unquestionably James is one of the most down-to-earth books in the New Testament. The writer is dealing with everyday affairs, covering such matters as one's speech, business ventures, the respect of persons, disagreements between Christian brethren, relations between employers and employees, and a number of other things. These are problems that touch our lives continually. The teaching of James, then, is designed to show the ways in which one's faith in God is not only tested to determine its genuineness, but applied to every area of human life.

Author

The writer of the book identifies himself as "James, a servant of God and of the Lord Jesus Christ" (1:1). As a number of men by this same name appear in the New Testament, brief consideration should be given to the problem. James, the son of Zebedee and the brother of John, was among the original disciples of the Lord Jesus. He was beheaded, however, by Herod Agrippa I (Acts 12:1, 2) before the year A.D. 44, and thus would not play a part in the history of the Jerusalem church during the time under consideration. James the son of Alphaeus was also one of Jesus' disciples (Matt. 10:3), but is not otherwise referred to in the narrative. Another of our Lord's disciples, Judas (not Iscariot), had a father whose name was James (Luke 6:16). But the only prominent figure by this name who continued through this period is the man called by Paul, "James, the Lord's brother" (Gal. 1:19). He appears in the Gospels as one of the four brothers of Christ (Matt. 13:55) and was, during Christ's ministry, an unbeliever (John 7:5). He is seen, however, as a believer in the Jerusalem prayer meeting (Acts 1:14; cf. 1 Cor. 15:7). Upon Peter's departure from Jerusalem, he assumes the leadership of the church there (Acts 12:17). A comparison of Galatians 2:9 with Acts 15:13-29 marks James as one of the pillars of the church. His final appearance in the New Testament is in Acts 21:18. According to tradition, James was martyred by the Jews in Jerusalem in A.D. 62.

Traditionally, this last of the four individuals has been known as the writer of the epistle bearing his name. He was a very devout man, deeply concerned about the careful regulation of the life of one who professed to believe in God. Known also as a man of prayer, he urged the same exercise upon his readers (cf. 5:16-18). His outlook is much the same as that found in the teaching of our Lord. Especially notable is the close similarity between this epistle and the Sermon on the Mount (Matt. 5-7).

What is faith? That is the question James attempts to answer. It is neither an academic nor an irrelevant inquiry. It is one that pierces to the depths of one's heart and to the center of his workaday world.

Outline

Purpose and Content

Surely it is worthy of notice that in an epistle dealing much with testing and suffering the opening words include "all joy" (1:2). Joy is a result of life with God. There are over four hundred instances of vocabulary relating to biblical joy. Joy comes from God and furthers the Christian's sanctification, especially during trials.

The chief purpose of trial is that it might bring about endurance (the literal meaning of "patience" in this passage) and completeness (1:3, 4). The word *temptation* (or trial) here has reference to outward pressures that bear hard upon the Christian. They are there by God's permission, designed to test (or prove) his faith and, when overcome, hold promise of reward (1:12). There is also the temptation that arises from within (1:13-15), due to man's own sinful nature, which does not come from God.

True faith is productive. This is due to its vital character—that which is alive is active. James discusses this important facet of truth under the subject of "faith and works" (2:14-26). The key statement is found in 2:14—"What *doth it* profit, my brethren, though a man say he hath faith, and have not works? can faith save him?" The expression "that faith" (ASV) has reference, not to faith in general, but a particular kind of faith, namely that which does not produce anything. James is saying if a man's life is barren of good works, we can only conclude that there is no genuine faith in God present. From the human point of view, then, faith must be shown to be known.

While this passage has often been set over against Paul's teaching about faith in Romans 4, the two really complement, rather than contradict, each other. In Romans, God knew that Abraham's faith was genuine because he looked on his heart; in James, men only knew Abraham's faith was genuine when they saw his good works as evidence. It seems that Paul himself puts the two elements together when he writes of faith working through love (Gal. 5:6).

James goes on from this point to show the relevance of all this to the life of one who professes to have faith in Christ. His injunctions such as on the use of the tongue (chap. 3), on business plans (chap. 4), and on prayer (chap. 5) are of a most practical nature.

HEBREWS

Theme

The central plea of this epistle is for the believer to "go on unto perfection" (6:1), not to digress or turn back to his former ways. On the one hand, solemn warnings are interspersed throughout the letter showing the danger of neglect, unbelief, immaturity, and apostasy. One is not to turn away from the truth and the privileges of the Gospel. On the other hand, the superiority of Christ is emphasized to a degree not found in any other book in the New Testament. He stands above men, angels, and ceremonies—He is the final revelation of God (1:2) and the mediator of a new and better covenant (8:6).

Authorship

One of the outstanding questions attached to Hebrews is the matter of authorship. The name of the author is absent from the letter, and all attempts to give a final answer have fallen short. Since about the fourth century the name of Paul has often been associated with it. One may point to the similarities with Paul's known epistles, such as the reference to Timothy (13:23); the request for prayer (13:18, 19; cf. Phil. 2:23, 24); the use of the phrase "the just shall live by faith" (10:38; cf. Rom. 1:17; Gal. 3:11), together with the great emphasis on the subject of faith.

Due to other features of the epistle, however, many have suggested other authors. The general style of the writing and the approach to the subject are not characteristically Pauline. The constant use of the Septuagint (the Greek version of the Old Testament) in quotations, the polished grammar, the view of the Law as "a shadow" (10:1) rather than "a curse" (Gal. 3:13), look away from Pauline authorship. Thus the names of Barnabas, Luke, and Apollos have all been suggested by scholars in early or later times. Usually such discussions end with the use of the famous statement by Origen of Alexandria (third century): "Who it was that wrote the epistle, God alone knows certainly."

Despite the uncertainty as to the human author, the grandeur of the epistle remains unmarred. It is a matchless presentation of the glories of Christ, the Redeemer, High Priest, and Changeless One (cf. 1:3; 2:17;

4:14-16; 7:25; 10:11-13; 13:8). The superiority of Christ and of the life of faith constitute the dual theme of the book.

Outline

The superiority of Christ	1:1–10:18
Above the prophets	1:1-3
Above the angels	1:4-14; 2:5-18
First warning—Neglect	2:1-4
Above Moses	3:1-6
Second warning—Unbelief	3:7-19
Above Joshua	4:2-10
Third warning—Unbelief	4:1, 11-13
Above Aaron	4:14–5:10
Fourth warning—Immaturity	5:11–6:20
Above the Levitical priesthood	7:1-28
Above the old covenant	8:1-13
Above the ordinances and sacrifices	9:1–10:18
The superiority of faith	10:19–13:21
The way of access to God	10:19-25
Fifth warning—Willful sin	10:26-31
The way of life in the world	10:32–11:40
The way of training as sons of God	12:1-13
Sixth warning—Apostasy	12:14-17
The way of heavenly privilege	12:18-24
Seventh warning—Refusal	12:25-29
The way of duty among men	13:1-21
Conclusion and Greetings	13:22-25

Purpose and Content

The opening statement of the epistle gathers the whole of the biblical revelation. God has spoken in the prophets—the Old Testament; and He has spoken in (His) Son—the New Testament. The very height of revelation came in the One who is also described as (1) Heir, (2) Creator, (3) Deity, (4) Preserver, and (5) Redeemer (1:2, 3). Now He resides at "the right hand of the throne of the Majesty in the heavens" as our High Priest (8:1).

Thus Christ appears as superior to the angels, for He is their Creator (1:4–2:18); to Moses and Joshua, for He is the Master over the servant (3:1–4:13); to Aaron and his successors, for He is the Great High Priest overshadowing the lesser priests (4:14–7:28). The New Covenant, of which Christ is mediator, is superior to the Old (8:1-13), and His sacrifice is superior to the ceremonial offerings of bulls and goats (9:1–10:18).[1]

The second major division (10:9–13:25) concerns faith as the superior way of life. Chapters 11 and 12 are especially outstanding here. The former shows in what ways the faith of the saints of the Old Testament was tested; the latter shows why our faith is tested. The "heroes of faith" showed what it meant to walk with God, to live and die in dependence on His promises. Christ is the greatest example of all—"the author and finisher of *our* faith" (12:2). We are to consider Him (12:3) and learn that God, in permitting trials and in chastising us, is dealing "with [us] as with sons" (12:7) to bring us to maturity and, ultimately, perfection.

Along with the two major emphases of the epistle are included the warning sections. While expositors differ as to precise interpretations, none fail to recognize the serious nature of these words. All the warnings could well be summed up in the words of 12:25, "See that ye refuse not him (God) that speaketh."[2]

Generally speaking, the warnings grow more severe and more climactic as the letter proceeds. The first warns of neglect (2:1-4); the last cautions against absolute refusal to heed what God has spoken (12:25-29). In terms of descriptive language, the two most harsh may well be those of 5:11–6:20 and 10:26-31. The one who "fell away" cannot be renewed to repentance; the one who "sins willfully" after knowing the truth is left without any sacrifice for sins.[3] The antidote to such perils is given in the exhortations of the book. There are thirteen expressions in all, urging the believer to grow in faith and to press forward instead of going backward in his spiritual experience (4:1, 11, 14, 16; 6:1; 10:22, 23, 24; 12:1 twice, 28; 13:13, 15).

1 PETER

Background

Written to "the strangers who scattered throughout Pontus, Galatia, Cappadocia, Asia, and Bithynia" (1:1), the first Epistle of Peter gives a ray of hope in the darkness to those suffering affliction and persecution. The word *suffering* is used ten times with reference to the lot of the Christian (2:19, 20; 3:14, 17; 4:1, 13, 15, 19; 5:9, 10).[4] In addition the word *temptation* or *trial* occurs in two crucial passages—1:6 and 4:12, respectively. What is the Christian to do and think in the face of such conditions? Peter's answer is given by his use of the word *hope,* found in 1:3, 13, 21; 3:5, 15, and by the assurance that God has a very definite purpose in permitting these difficulties in our lives.

Author

The name Peter is one already familiar to the reader of the historical books of the New Testament. He played a major part in the earthly ministry of our Lord and was the leader of the Jerusalem church in the first twelve chapters of Acts. A fisherman of Bethsaida, close to the Sea of Galilee in northern Palestine (John 1:44), Peter was the older brother of Andrew. He was first brought to Jesus by his brother (John 1:40-42), and it was prophesied by the Lord at that time that the old, unstable Simon would one day be the new, rock-like Peter. Peter was called from his fishing boat to become a fisher of men (Mark 1:16-18; Luke 5:1-11). Finally, in Mark 3:13-16, he was called and chosen as one of the Twelve to accompany the Lord and to carry on an evangelistic ministry. As one of the inner circle, together with James and John, he accompanied Christ at a number of important events: the raising of Jairus' daughter (Luke 8:54); the Transfiguration scene (Luke 9:28); and on the crucifixion eve in the Garden of Gethsemane (Matt. 26:37). Being overconfident regarding his undying loyalty to his Lord, Peter soon denied Him (John 13:36-38; 18:15-27), but was afterward graciously restored to fellowship and commissioned to follow and serve Christ once again (1 Cor. 15:5; John 21:15-19). As the leader of the early church in Jerusalem, Peter appears as a fearless preacher, defender, and administrator. That he did learn his lesson is evident from the reading of this letter. It abounds with references to faithfulness, the care of a shepherd for the sheep, and the responsibilities of the Christian toward his Lord and his fellow Christians. Thus, out of a full life, Peter, now an old man, writes to believers who are beset by trials and sufferings. He had found the Lord sufficient; now he exhorts these people to cast all their anxieties upon Him because He cares for them (5:7).

Outline

Salutation	1:1, 2
Perspective and suffering	1:3–2:10
Pressure and suffering	2:11–4:6
Service and suffering	4:7-11
Witness and suffering	4:12-19
Personal attitudes and suffering	5:1-11
Conclusion	5:12-14

Purpose and Content

The Christian life is never described as a bed of roses. In fact, Peter states, amid the sufferings that were then present, "For even hereunto were ye called: because Christ also suffered for us, leaving us an example, that ye should follow in his steps" (2:21). For what reasons are such things permitted by the Lord? They are meant to prove our faith that we may "be found unto praise and honour and glory at the appearing of Jesus Christ" (1:7). It is actually a privilege to "suffer for righteousness' sake" (3:14); our Lord has suffered on this account (2:21; 4:1). Partaking of Christ's sufferings will result in rejoicing at His coming (4:13). There is suffering that is "according to the will of God," which is meant to bring a committal of our souls "in well doing, as unto a faithful Creator" (4:19). That is to say, God knows what He is doing. We are to continue to do well despite our circumstances. We have been called as God's children to share His glory. He Himself shall "make you perfect, stablish, strengthen, settle *you*" (5:10).

Countering this emphasis is the note of hope.[5] What comfort this affords to the Christian. God has begotten us "unto a living hope" (1:3), and has reserved an inheritance for us in heaven (1:4), and is guarding us in view of that day (1:5). Our hope is on the grace of God and on God Himself (1:13, 21; 3:5). Even as He raised Christ from the dead, so we also shall be caught up to glory. The hope within us, being laid hold of by faith, becomes so real that people around us inquire concerning it (3:15). Thus the very hardships we face become opportunities for witnessing for Christ.

Peter's use of the imperative mood of the verb in his epistle is noteworthy, together with participles used in the sense of commands. By such devices he has attempted to impress upon his readers that living for God makes real demands upon us. This positive injunction is to guide us and form us unto the day of Christ's appearing.[6] It is an application of Christ's word in the second Gospel, "Thou shalt love the Lord thy God with all thy heart, and with all thy soul, and with all thy mind, and with all thy strength . . . (and) thou shalt love thy neighbour as thyself" (Mark 12:30, 31). We show our love by obeying His commands (cf. 1 Pet. 1:22).

DISCUSSION QUESTIONS

1. On what important subject is James a treatise?
2. According to James, what are some aspects of daily living that should be affected by our faith?
3. Give a brief background of the probable writer of the book of James.
4. Compare and show the relationship of James's teaching on faith with Paul's teaching on the subject in Romans 4.

5. In what ways is the book of Hebrews similar to Paul's known epistles?
6. What is the dual theme of the book of Hebrews?
7. To whom is Christ considered superior in the book of Hebrews?
8. Briefly summarize the ministry of Peter prior to Christ's death.
9. Summarize Peter's teaching concerning suffering as found in 1 Peter.

APPLICATION ACTIVITIES

1. Compare and contrast the lives of Peter and James.
2. What important lessons should be learned from the warnings of Hebrews?
3. List some practical problems found in most Christians' lives that are answered in these epistles. Indicate where each answer is found.
4. To understand more fully the differences between "law" and "grace" or "faith" and "works," expand activity #2 of chapter 7 by indicating specific contrasts between them in the book of Hebrews.
5. Prepare a summary of the character and ministry of Christ as presented in the book of Hebrews. -OR- Expand your chart prepared for chapter 1, activity #1.
6. List the characteristics of today's true Christian as portrayed in these epistles.

THE CHURCH AND FALSE TEACHING

2 Peter, Jude, 1, 2, and 3 John

The last five New Testament Epistles, three of them containing only one brief chapter each, are linked together by their common concern with false teaching in the realm of Christian doctrine and ethics. Second Peter and Jude warn against those who scorn the authority of the Lord and His Word. Like false teachers in the Old Testament, they will taste the judgment of God coming upon them. The three letters ascribed to John, though like Hebrews in their anonymity, are written against the malignant influence of Gnosticism, which at this date (late first century) was beginning to show itself as a system of teaching. Professing to possess superior, mystic knowledge leading to salvation, the teaching of the Gnostics set forth strange views of Christ and the nature of creation. John calls it the "*spirit* of antichrist" (1 John 4:1-3).

2 PETER

Authorship

The early church was slow in acknowledging 2 Peter to be on the same level with the other books that came to compose the New Testament canon. A number of contrasts with 1 Peter are readily noticed, such as the lack of specific address (as in 1 Pet. 1:1), the rough grammatical character and style of writing, and in addition, the striking similarities of language between chapter 2 and the Epistle of Jude. Yet it should be remembered that the book was recognized as canonical by the Council of Laodicea in A.D. 363 and the Council of Carthage in A.D. 397.

The internal evidence for Petrine authorship is much more definite. The writer calls himself "Simon Peter, a servant and apostle of Jesus Christ" (1:1). The name Simon (or Simeon) is reminiscent of Peter's original name (cf. John 1:42; Acts 15:14). There are many autobiographical references in the letter. The author recalls the Transfiguration experience (1:16-18; cf. Mark 9:2-8). He uses a fisherman's word, *enticing*, in 2:14, 18 (ASV). In 3:1, he makes reference to this letter as "this second epistle" he had written to these readers. Further, he is one with his readers in having obtained similarly precious faith.

Theme

The key word of the epistle is *knowledge*, which occurs twelve times in its various forms (1:2, 3, 5, 6, 8, 16, 20; 2:20, 21; 3:3, 17, 18). In a letter that aims to combat false teaching, the knowledge of the truth is the key idea. Together with this, Peter stresses the importance of remembering certain things (1:12, 13; 3:1) and shows the danger of forgetting important truths (1:9; 3:8). Thus, throughout the letter, the teachings of the Word of God are represented as true and normative for the Christian life.

Outline

Introduction	1:1, 2
Knowledge and the Christian life	1:3-11
Knowledge and the Word of God	1:12-21
Knowledge and the false teaching	2:1-22
Knowledge and the Second Coming	3:1-13
Conclusion—Steadfastness and growth	3:14-18

Purpose and Content

God has made full provision for the spiritual life of the believer (1:3). Thus, the believer's responsibility is to avail himself of the divine resources so that he will be neither "barren nor unfruitful in the knowledge of our Lord Jesus Christ" (1:8). This is Peter's opening thought in the epistle, and by means of these statements he prepares the way for his main arguments.

First, the Word of God given by the Holy Spirit (1:20, 21) is that to which we should give heed (1:19). Because its source is divine, its message is authoritative. It should be stressed that the chief thrust of the statement in 1:20, 21 is regarding the origin, not the meaning, of Scripture. It came not "by the will of man" but "by the Holy Ghost."

Second, the path taken by the false teachers, who deny "the Lord that bought them," leads toward certain judgment (2:1) and "the latter end is worse with them than the beginning" (2:20). Those who follow them can expect nothing better. The sure judgment of God upon the sinners of the Old Testament (2:4, 5, 6, 15) is a solemn warning to all.

Third, the Second Coming of Christ will be God's vindication of His name and purpose, and "the day of the Lord" will be the day of judgment for the scoffers of the world (chap. 3). Those who deny the reality of this event forget "this one thing," says Peter, "that one day is with the Lord as a thousand years, and a thousand years as one day" (3:8). Only because God is longsuffering, "not willing that any should perish," do the scoffers even remain to carry on their false ways (3:9).

This final message leaves a challenge with the readers of the letter. "Wherefore, beloved, seeing that ye look for such things, be diligent that ye may be found of him in peace, without spot, and blameless . . . But grow in grace, and in the knowledge of our Lord and Savior Jesus Christ. To him *be* the glory both now and for ever" (3:14, 18).

JUDE

The letter that was to have been written concerning "our common faith" turned out, by constraint upon the writer, to be an exhortation to "earnestly contend for the faith" (v. 3). One of the chief differences between Jude and 2 Peter seems to be that while Peter warned that "there shall be false teachers" (2:1), Jude states that "there are certain men crept in unawares" (v. 4). One anticipates the problem, while the other realizes it as a present reality. Apparently, then, this epistle is somewhat later than 2 Peter. If Peter is dated about A.D. 65-67, Jude might be placed at A.D. 75-85.

Author

Jude was a "brother of James" and seems to fit into the pattern sketched earlier (chapter ten of James). Christ and James were recorded as having a brother named Jude (Matt. 13:55). James and Jude along with Jesus' other brothers appear as believers in Acts 1:14, and the author writes now as "a servant of Jesus Christ" (Jude 1).

Theme

As he begins to write, the author uses the interesting expression, "the faith which was once delivered unto the saints" (v. 3).[1] Here "the faith" has reference to "the body of doctrine" held in common by the church at that time. There is a note of finality about it—"which was once delivered." God has committed the Gospel to the church to be kept inviolate, as a trust (cf. Gal. 1:6-9; 1 Tim. 1:19; 6:3, 20, 21; 2 Tim. 1:13, 14). Doctrine, however, is not to be held in detachment from life. Correct teaching must result in holy living, else the practical purpose is lost. This is the error Jude combats—a kind of antinomianism or lawless libertinism that results in a denial of the rightful place of Christ in the life of the individual (v. 4).

Outline

Salutation	1, 2
Exhortation—Defense of the faith	3, 4
Illustration—Departures from the faith	5-16
Admonition—Progress in the faith	17-23
Conclusion—A doxology	24, 25

Purpose and Content

Jude, along with 2 Peter 2, turns to the Old Testament for illustrations of godlessness and makes clear God's judgment upon all such persons. A comparison of the two is as follows.

Ref.	Jude	Ref.	2 Peter 2
v. 5	Israel in the wilderness	___	_____
v. 6	The angels who fell	v. 4	The angels who fell
___	_____	v. 5	Sodom and Gomorrah
v. 11	The way of Cain	___	_____
v. 11	The error of Balaam	v. 15	The way of Balaam
v. 11	The disputing of Korah	___	_____

Jude employed these illustrations for a number of specific reasons.

First, he used them as a means of informing his readers of the serious consequences of unbelief. Israel illustrates unbelief (v. 5); the fallen angels illustrate disobedience (v. 6); Sodom and Gomorrah illustrate moral defilement (v. 7).

Second, Jude thus depicted the character of the false teachers of whom he warns his readers. Cain is a picture of willfulness, Balaam of greed, and Korah of presumption (v. 11).[2]

Third, by way of anticipation, Jude tells what will be the end of the false teachers. Using a quotation from the Jewish work, *The Book of Enoch,* he illustrates what God will do to these "ungodly sinners" (v. 14, 15).

In the face of all such dangers, the personal responsibility of the believer is (1) to remember the apostles' teaching (v. 17) and (2) to keep himself in the love of God (v. 21). This latter injunction is linked with a number of participial clauses: (a) building himself up in most holy faith (v. 20), (b) praying in the Holy Spirit (v. 20), and (c) looking for the mercy of our Lord Jesus Christ unto eternal life (v. 21). Along with these, the believer's responsibility to others is (1) to have mercy on some (v. 22, 23) and (2) to save some out of the fire (v. 23).

1 JOHN

Background

John writes against the Gnostics who denied the reality of our Lord's humanity as well as His deity. John's epistles, especially the first, are powerful weapons against such heresies, whether in old or modern dress.

This letter is closely related to his Gospel (see chapter 4). Both concern the Lord Jesus and the eternal life that comes to those who trust in Him (John 20:30, 31; 1 John 5:13). The Gospel gives the declaration of salvation; the letter, the assurance of it. Both speak of "the Word," the term used for Christ as the revealer of God.[3] The vocabulary of the books is similar, both employing such important words as *beginning* (cf. 1:1 in each); *witness* (thirty-three times in John, six times in 1 John); *believe* (ninety-eight times and nine times); *eternal life* (John 3:15; 1 John 1:2); *love* (John 3:16; 1 John 4:9); *abide* (John 15:4; 1 John 2:28); and many others.

All of John's writings are usually dated near the end of the first century, somewhere between A.D. 85-95. Thus, as an old man, he looks back to his experiences with his Lord, upon which he had long meditated, and also at the current problems of the church.

Purpose and Content

John writes to define the nature of the person of Christ in the face of heretical teachings afflicting the church near the end of the first century. The general name given to this teaching was Gnosticism, a religiophilosophic school basically characterized by the idea that only spirit was good and matter was evil. As in other Greek and Oriental religious systems, the Gnostics believed that one must free himself from the material world and be occupied alone with spirit. The way of escape, for the Gnostics, was the way of superior knowledge. By learning the mysterious secrets of the universe, the initiate of the cult could supposedly attain freedom.

With regard to the teachings of Christianity, the opposition of this heresy centered in the person of Christ. Obviously, if matter (which involved the human body) was evil, God could not be manifest in the flesh, else He would be defiled. Therefore, Christ's humanity was not real; the disciples only saw a phantom; Christ only seemed to be real. If, as others taught, Jesus was truly man, the Christ-spirit did not actually unite with Him, except for the brief time between the baptism and the crucifixion.[4] This was, therefore, a denial of His deity.

When one becomes aware of these prevalent false claims, many of

John's statements in the first epistle take on new meaning. John combats Docetism (see note 4) by his insistence on the reality of the humanity of Christ (1:1-3; 4:1-3). He utters severe words against Cerinthianism (see note 4) by emphasizing the fact that Jesus is the Christ, the Son of God (1:3, 7; 2:22, 23; 3:23; 4:15; 5:1, 20). This epistle should serve as a final answer to a heresy that persists until the present day.

The primary purpose of the epistle, as stated by John himself, is given in 5:13: "These things have I written unto you . . . that ye may know that ye have eternal life, and that ye may believe on the name of the Son of God." His remarks are addressed to "the children of God," those who have been "begotten of God." Thus it is a family letter and the word *fellowship* is used by John to describe the ideal relationship between God and His children (cf. 1:3, 6, 7).

Outline

Introduction—The reality of fellowship	1:1-4
The requirements for fellowship	1:5-10
The victorious character of fellowship	2:1-17
The enemies of fellowship	2:18-29
The reasons for fellowship	3:1-12
The tests of fellowship	3:13-24
The discernment of fellowship	4:1-6
The practice of fellowship	4:7-21
The foundation of fellowship	5:1-12
The privileges of fellowship	5:13-21

Characteristic Features

In this letter, John describes God as "light" (1:5) and "love" (4:8). "Light" has reference to God's holiness (cf. James 1:17) and is meant to stress to the believer the need for properly dealing with any sin in his life, that is, anything that would prevent fellowship with his Father. In 1:5–2:2 the remedy is given. The blood of Christ is the basis for cleansing (1:7); confession on the part of the believer is the condition for cleansing (1:9); and forgiveness by God is the accompaniment of cleansing (1:9). Those who deny the presence of a sin nature (1:8) only deceive themselves; those who deny they have committed acts of sin (1:10) make God a liar.

The other descriptive word, *love*, refers to God's attitude toward us, and describes His nature (cf. 4:9). We learn the meaning of love by seeing what God has done for us (4:10). As a result of observing God's love, we are not only to love Him, but one another also (4:11).

Notice that John, as he writes, makes use of many contrasting terms and ideas. Things are "either black or white." He speaks in terms of "one or the other." Such passages as 1:6, 7; 2:4, 5; 2:9, 10; 2:17; 2:22, 23; 3:10, 18; 4:2, 3, 20; and 5:12 are outstanding examples of his technique. John's epistle is written to enable us to put our profession to the test.

Among all the New Testament writers, only John uses the now familiar expression "Antichrist." It is introduced in 1 John 2:18, then appears in 2:22; 4:3; and 2 John 7. The meaning of *anti* is "one who takes the place of" or "one who stands against (or opposes)." The essence of the nature of the Antichrist is the denial of the rightful place of the Father and the Son; the Antichrist himself would be supreme in the world. Furthermore, the spirit of antichrist is a denial of the reality of Christ's incarnation, thus attempting to do away with Christ's redemptive work, by which He laid the sentence of death upon Satan himself (cf. Heb. 2:14). "And we know that the Son of God is come, and hath given us an understanding, that we may know him that is true, and we are in him that is true, *even* in his Son" (1 John 5:20).

2 JOHN

Purpose and Content

Second John, together with 3 John, seems to be a sampling of John's personal correspondence. Both letters are addressed to individuals and have to do with a number of personal matters.

The key word of the letter is *truth.* John stresses the need for "walking in the truth" (v. 4) because "many deceivers are entered into the world" (v. 7). He who denies the doctrine of Christ is not to be given Christian greetings, lest we find ourselves partaking in "his evil deeds" (v. 10, 11).

Outline

Salutation	1-3
Walking in the truth	4-11
The commandment of the Father	4-6
The message of the deceivers	7-11
Conclusion	12, 13

3 JOHN

Purpose and Content

The recipient of this final epistle of John is called only "well-beloved Gaius" (v. 1). He is identified no further, so must have been well known to the members of the Asian churches where John served during the last years of his life. The name itself was a familiar one, often appearing in the writings of Paul, where we see Gaius (of Corinth) in Romans

16:23, Paul's host in that city; Gaius of Macedonia in Acts 19:29; and Gaius of Derbe in Acts 20:4.

Third John's main theme is hospitality. The letter recognizes the kindnesses of Gaius in showing an open door to Christian workers and strangers alike (v. 5) and encourages him to continue this ministry (v. 6).

John promises to discipline the troublesome Diotrephes, who brazenly excommunicated those in the church who did not recognize his "preeminence" (v. 9, 10). By way of contrast, the man Demetrius is commended by all in the church (v. 12). John's commendation, "good report of all *men*, and of the truth itself," challenges the Christian to walk in truth.

Outline

Salutation	1
Prayer for Gaius' health	2-4
Praise for Gaius' hospitality	5-8
Condemnation of Diotrephes' policy	9-11
Commendation of Demetrius' character	12
Conclusion	13

DISCUSSION QUESTIONS

1. What emphasis is common among the last five New Testament Epistles?
2. How is the theme of 2 Peter emphasized by the writer?
3. What is the teaching of 2 Peter concerning the Scriptures?
4. Compare 2 Peter and Jude in reference to their statements concerning false teachers.
5. What illustrations of Old Testament godlessness are used by both Peter and Jude?
6. Compare the similarities of emphases by John in 1 John and his Gospel.
7. Justify calling 1 John a family letter.
8. What attitudes and teachings characterize the spirit of antichrist?
9. What was John's purpose in writing 2 and 3 John?

APPLICATION ACTIVITIES

1. Show from 1 John the tests by which a person today can know whether or not he is truly a Christian.
2. Compare present-day error with Gnosticism and indicate how 1 John provides answers for those denying Christ's deity or bodily existence.
3. From 2 Peter and 1 John, expand your findings on the true Christian in chapter 10, activity #6.
4. Without the use of aids, prepare an outline for one of the epistles studied in this chapter.

BOOK OF THE REVELATION

The book of Revelation, like the book of Daniel in the Old Testament, is apocalyptic. The term "apocalyptic" means "to unveil" or "to uncover;" thus, "to reveal" something that has been beforehand veiled, covered, or hidden. Several characteristics of apocalyptic writing are worthy of mention. Apocalyptic writing . . .

Is usually written in times of trouble and distress

This is seen in both Daniel and Revelation. In Daniel, the days of the Babylonian captivity are vividly portrayed. In Revelation, the central issue is the beginnings of the conflict between the Roman Empire and the Church.

Conveys its message by means of signs, symbols, dreams, and visions

John writes in Revelation 1:1 that his message was "sent and signified" (i.e., portrayed by the use of "signs," or physical figures having spiritual meanings attached to them). Within the framework of four great visions, John presents the main outlines of his message.

Gives promise of the eventual triumph of good over evil

By the appearance of the kingdom of God, together with the heavenly Lord (cf. "KING OF KINGS AND LORD OF LORDS," Rev. 19:16) as the sovereign ruler of the creation, all things shall be subjected to God's will (cf. Dan. 2:44; Rev. 11:15).

Despite the fact that the Revelation seems to many to be strange and foreboding, and thus is often neglected, the Revelation is the only book in the New Testament containing the promise of blessing to "he that readeth, and they that hear the words of this prophecy, and keep those things which are written therein" (1:3; cf. Josh. 1:7, 8). In addition, the book closes with a serious warning to any who would add to or take away from the contents of the prophecy (22:18, 19). Above all, it must be emphasized that this book is, according to its own statement, "the

Revelation of Jesus Christ, which God gave unto him, to shew unto his servants" (1:1). With such character attached to it by so plain a statement, the contents are worthy of the diligent study of every believer.

Background

By reading the book itself, one sees readily that persecution and trouble were already threatening the Church. Serious problems were in evidence both from without and within. The church of Ephesus was commended for her endurance and discernment of evil men (2:2); the church of Smyrna would have tribulation ten days (2:10); in Pergamum, Antipas was martyred (2:13); "great tribulation" hung over Thyatira (2:22); and the church in Philadelphia was promised the Lord's protection amid the hour of trial (3:10).

The date of the writing of Revelation was about A.D. 90-95. During the first century, the Roman emperors held sway over the world, from Augustus to Domitian. All the Roman persecutions before the days of the Emperor Decius (A.D. 250) were local in nature. The Christians in certain places began to feel the sting of official opposition in A.D. 64, then again, it seems, during Domitian's time. The exile of John to Patmos was just one example of the present and impending tribulations spoken of within the Revelation (1:9).

Would this be the lot of the Church forever? Was it possible that Satan and his evil agents would win the victory? The book gives a decisive answer. The dragon would be cast down from heaven (12:9), and the saints would overcome him (12:11). Eventually, the dragon and his kind would be cast into "the lake of fire" (19:20; 20:10). Thus, God would be supreme and the Church established forever, "as a bride adorned for her husband" (21:2). Even as the Lord Jesus had said, so it would be: "the gates of hell shall not prevail against it" (Matt. 16:18).

Methods of Interpretation

Before attempting to investigate the details of the book, it is necessary to establish some methods of approaching it. Bible scholars recognize four basic methods.

The preterist method

This approach asserts that the events in Revelation belong to the first century, and have, therefore, long ago been fulfilled. It maintains a past perspective. There is no prophetic or future aspect to the book. According to the preterist method, the setting for the visions was the existing conflict between the Church and Rome in the age of the apostles (i.e., up to A.D. 100).

This view emphasizes the relevance of the book to the churches to which it was written (1:11), but it hardly seems in keeping with the professed forward look of John's message, which specifically presents predictions of things to come (cf. 1:3, 19; 22:18, 19).

The historicist method

This approach sees the Revelation as a picture book of the conflict between the Church and the world (energized by Satan) from the time of the apostles until the end of the age. The approach gives full recognition to the relationship between the drama of the book and earthly events. The crises that have arisen in world history—the conquerors of past and present—are portrayed herein, and all are doomed to failure.

The major weakness of this method is the difficulty in equating events of the book with events in history. Serious and apparently irreconcilable disagreements between those who hold the view cast doubt upon the validity of the approach as a single solution to the book. Yet it does stress the tangency of the message to the realm of human history.

The futurist method

With the exception of chapters 1-3, Revelation is viewed as wholly futuristic, depicting the drama that awaits the end of the age, the day of God's wrath and the appearance of Christ from heaven. The opening section of the book, the letters to the seven churches (chap. 1-3), is either regarded as limited to the first century or as a kind of sevenfold, symbolic sketch of the spiritual history of the Church from the apostolic age to the Second Advent.

In view of the prophetic language of the book (4:1) and the magnitude of the events predicted in chapters 4-22, this method seems to do greater justice to the interpretation than the previous methods. Yet the possible danger is that the book is thus rendered irrelevant to the first-century recipients of its message and, in a sense, to anyone prior to the end of the age itself. If this tendency is guarded against, the futurist method is of great value.

The idealist method

This method should be distinguished from the three that have been discussed in that it is not tied to history, that is, the occurrence of literal events. It deals with spiritual, rather than historical, realities. Emphasizing the conflict between God and Satan, good and evil, righteousness and sin, it assures the reader, apart from concern with specific historical situations, that the victory will be won by the forces of right.

Certainly the spirit of the book has been caught by the idealist approach, but the virtual elimination of the historical setting is hardly in keeping with the biblical teaching of God's activity within the realm of human history. The symbolic element should not be the single emphasis; the predictive aspect must be maintained.

None of these approaches to the interpretation of this prophecy is singularly satisfactory. An attempt has been made to state concisely the strengths and weaknesses of all the methods, thus enabling students to cull from each the useful features and use them wisely in their own study. In this task, as in all Bible study, the guidance of the Holy Spirit is essential (1 Cor. 2:6-16; James 1:5).

Structure of the Book

In analyzing the Revelation with regard to its structure, notice that John uses a key phrase four times, thus dividing the book into major divisions based upon four visions that he saw. The phrase "in the Spirit" occurs in 1:10; 4:2; 17:3; and 21:10. It is used in the Old Testament regarding the prophets as they experienced the revelatory ministry of the Holy Spirit, conveying to them the Word of God (cf. Ezek. 3:12; 37:1). The chart that follows will aid in identifying the visions as they appear throughout the book.

Ref.	Location	Vision	Content
1:9–3:22	Patmos	One like unto a Son of Man	Christ as Lord amidst His churches
4:1–16:21	Heaven	The Throne and the Lamb	Christ as the Lamb; wrath of God
17:1–21:8	Wilderness	A Woman and the Beast	Christ as King of Kings and Victor over His enemies
21:9–22:6	Mountain	The New Jerusalem	Christ as Bridegroom with His bride in glory

Outline

The outline for the book is built around the four visions, together with the introduction (1:1-8) and the conclusion (22:6-21). It emphasizes the centrality of Christ throughout the entire portrayal.

Introduction	1:1-8
The first vision—Christ and the seven churches	1:9–3:22

The first vision, in one sense, is easier to understand than those that follow. As the Lord speaks to John (1:9-20) and then to the seven churches (chap. 2, 3), we find language that, within the context of first-century conditions, is relatively clear. Emphasized here is the sovereignty of the Head as He walks among the lampstands (the churches) and holds the seven stars (the messengers, or leaders, of the churches) within His right hand, the place of authority and honor.

The seven churches of Asia, selected from a greater number then existing, are each analyzed by the Lord, and their spiritual condition is laid bare.[1] Christ follows a general pattern in speaking to each. Two exceptions are notable, however. Each church (as a whole) is commended except two, Sardis and Laodicea. Each church (as a whole) is condemned except two, Smyrna and Philadelphia.[2] The careful study of each letter, giving attention to the background and location of each church, the kinds of things said to each, and the spiritual counsel for the present day, will prove most rewarding.

The framework for the second vision (4:1–16:21) is the description of the three series of judgments upon the earth, each consisting of seven parts.[3] The magnitude of these events is breathtaking, and, whether interpreted literally or symbolically, they impress the reader with the fury of divine vengeance against unrepentant sinners (cf. Rom. 12:19; Heb. 10:30, 31).

In considering the three series of judgments, attention should be called to the problem of the relation of the judgments. Briefly it is this, do they follow one another (consecutive)? Do they occur within the same period of time and end together (concurrent)? Or, do they all happen at the same time (simultaneous)? Each of the three positions has been adopted by equally sound commentators; no final solution has yet appeared.

Within this general framework a number of parenthetical events occur. They are found in 7:1-8; 7:9-17; 10:1-11; 11:1-13; 12:1-17; 13:1-18; 14:1-5; 14:6-12; 14:13; 14:14-20. These events, for the most part, appear to occur within the same time sequence as the judgments, but concentrate mainly upon persons, both human and angelic, showing their relation to the day of God's wrath.

The third vision (17:1–21:8) gives special attention to the victory of Christ over His enemies. In order of occurrence they are the harlot and the Beast of Babylon; the Beast and the false prophets with their followers; Satan and the rebels of earth; and unregenerate mankind. Thus the way is prepared for "the new heavens and the new earth." A crucial passage within this vision is 20:4-6, picturing the millennial reign of Christ, when He shall be vindicated upon the earth, the place of His rejection (cf. 1 Cor. 15:25-27). The saints shall reign with Him (cf. 1 Cor. 6:2) and shall exercise their function as "priests of God and of Christ."

Finally, in the fourth vision (21:9–22:5) dawns "the new heavens and the new earth." The spotless bride of Christ stands in vivid contrast to the scarlet woman, the harlot of Babylon (chap. 17). The perfections of the New Jerusalem are portrayed by John, centered in the unbroken fellowship between God and His people. With the banishment of death and the appearance of the tree of life, the pristine beauty of Eden reappears (cf. Gen. 2). That which sin has defiled is here restored and purified. Thus God shall be "all in all." The story of redemption is completed.

DISCUSSION QUESTIONS

1. List and illustrate from the Revelation three outstanding characteristics of apocalyptic writings.
2. Why is this book worthy of the diligent study of every believer?
3. Within what framework does John present the main outlines of his message?
4. Give a brief background for John's writing the book of Revelation.
5. Define and comment briefly on four methods of interpreting the Revelation.
6. What three possible views concerning the judgments divide Bible scholars?

7. What enemies of Christ are defeated in Revelation 17-20 in order to prepare the way for the new heavens and the new earth?

8. Briefly summarize the blessings of Revelation 21 and 22.

APPLICATION ACTIVITIES

1. Compare the presentation of the character of Christ in the letters to the seven churches with the depiction of Him in the Epistles.

2. Justify dividing the book into four sections on the basis of the phrase "in the Spirit." Compare our use of the term today.

3. From your Scripture reading give a brief account of the final events and doom of Satan and his followers.

4. Write a paper of several paragraphs summarizing the message of the New Testament as it applies to your own life.

The Missionary Journeys of Paul

References	Places Visited	Personnel	Main Events	Main Results

First Journey
Acts 13:4–14:28
	Departure from Antioch (Syria)
	Seleucia
	Cyprus: Salamis
	    Paphos
	Pamphylia: Perga
	Galatia: Antioch
	    Iconium
	    Lystra
	    Derbe
	Return to Antioch (Syria)
		Paul
		Barnabas
		John Mark
			Contest with Elymas at Paphos
			Sermon in synagogue at Antioch (Pisidia)
			Paul and Barnabas worshiped at Lystra
			Paul preaches, then is stoned at Lystra
				Conversion of Sergius Paulus at Paphos
				Conversions and riot at Antioch (Pisidia)
				Churches founded and established in all Galatian cities; elders appointed
				Report of journey to the church in Antioch (Syria)

Second Journey
Acts 15:36–18:22
	Departure from Antioch (Syria)
	Syria and Cilicia
	Galatia: Derbe and Lystra
	Troas
	Macedonia: Philippi
	    Thessalonica
	    Berea
	Achaia: Athens
	    Corinth
	Caesarea
	Return to Antioch (Syria)
		Paul
		Silas
		Timothy
		(Luke)
			Timothy added to party at Lystra
			Vision at Troas; Luke added to party
			Preaching and imprisonment at Philippi
			Preaching and persecution at Thessalonica
			Preaching at Berea
			Sermon on Mars' Hill in Athens
			Eighteen-month stay at Corinth, teaching, trial before Gallio
			Short stay at Ephesus, preaching
				Conversion of Lydia and the jailer at Philippi; church founded
				Church founded at Thessalonica
				Conversion of Dionysius and Damaris at Athens
				Church founded at Corinth

Third Journey Acts 18:23–21:14	Departure from Antioch (Syria) Galatia and Phrygia Asia: Ephesus Macedonia Greece Macedonian cities Troas Asia: Melitus Syria: Tyre Ptolemais Caesarea Jerusalem	Paul Silas Timothy (Luke) Gaius Aristarchus Sopater Secundus Tychicus Trophimus	Teaching ministry in Ephesus (2–3 years) Riot of the Ephesian silversmiths Preaching at Troas Eutychus restored to life Farewell to the Ephesian elders at Miletus Warning to Paul at Tyre regarding Jerusalem Warning to Paul at Caesarea by Agabus regarding Jerusalem	Church established at Ephesus; center of evangelization of Asia Instruction to the Ephesian elders regarding official duties

The Letters to the Seven Churches of Asia

Church	Ephesus 2:1-7	Smyrna 2:8-11	Pergamum 2:12-17	Thyatira 2:18-29	Sardis 3:1-6	Philadelphia 3:7-13	Laodicea 3:14-22
Character of Christ	Sovereign Lord 2:1	Risen Lord 2:8	Warring Lord 2:12, 16	Judging Lord 2:18	Omniscient Lord 3:1	Authoritative Lord 3:7	Divine Lord 3:14
Commendation	Orthodoxy 2:2	Endurance 2:9	Faithfulness 2:13	Industry 2:19	(none) 3:1	Endurance 3:10	(none)
Condemnation	Coldness 2:4	(none)	False Teaching 2:14, 15	Unfaithfulness 2:20	Unreality 3:1	(none)	Lukewarmness 3:15, 16
Counsel	Remember, repent, repeat first works 2:5	Be watchful unto death 2:10	Repent 2:16	Repent; hold fast 2:22, 25	Be watchful; remember, repent 3:2, 3	Hold fast 3:11	Buy gold, garments, eyesalve 3:18, 19
Caution	Removal 2:5	(none)	War 2:16	Death 2:23	Invasion 3:3	(none)	Separation 3:16
Covenant with Overcomer	Eat of the tree of life 2:7	Not hurt by the second death 2:11	Hidden manna, white stone, new name 2:17	Rulership; morning star 2:26-28	White garments; name kept and confessed 3:5	New position; new name 3:12	Share Christ's throne 3:21

The Three Series of Judgments

	Seal Judgments	Trumpet Judgments	Vial Judgments
1	6:1, 2 Rider on a white horse Carried a bow Wore a crown *Object:* To conquer	8:7 Hail, fire, and blood on the earth *Result:* 1/3 part earth, 1/3 part trees, all green grass burned up	16:2 Poured into earth *Result:* Noisome and grievous sore upon worshipers of the Beast
2	6:3, 4 Rider on a red horse Carried a great sword *Object:* To take peace from the earth	8:8, 9 Fiery mountain cast into the sea *Result:* 1/3 of sea blood, 1/3 of sea creatures die, 1/3 of ships destroyed	16:3 Poured into the sea *Result:* All sea-life died
3	6:5, 6 Rider on a black horse Carried a balance *Object:* Produce famine conditions	8:10, 11 Burning star falls upon earth—named Wormwood *Result:* 1/3 of waters made bitter; many men die	16:4-7 Poured in rivers and sources of waters *Result:* Water became blood; revenge on murderers
4	6:7, 8 Rider on a pale horse Death followed by Hades *Object:* To kill by sword, famine, death, and wild beasts	8:12 Celestial disturbances *Result:* 1/3 of heavenly bodies darkened; day and night affected	16:8, 9 Poured upon the sun *Result:* Men scorched with fire; blasphemed God
5	6:9-11 Souls of martyrs under the altar *Object:* To cry for revenge against their murderers	9:1-11 Star (ruler) falls to earth; opens the pit; locusts emerge, led by Apollyon *Result:* Men tormented 5 months; unable to die	16:10, 11 Poured upon the throne of the beast *Result:* Kingdom darkened; men in pain; did not repent
6	6:12-17 Seismic and celestial disturbances *Object:* Day of God's wrath upon the earth	9:13-22 Four angels at Euphrates released; armies of horsemen proceed *Result:* 1/3 of men killed by horses that breathe fire, smoke, and brimstone	16:12-16 Poured upon Euphrates River *Result:* River dried up; eastern kings advance to Har-Magedon (Armageddon)
7	8:1, 2 Silence in heaven for a half-hour *Object:* Preparation for sounding of seven trumpets	11:15-19 Great voices in heaven and 24 elders sing praise to God *Result:* God's kingdom supreme over the earth	16:17-21 Poured upon the air *Result:* Voice announces "It is done;" disturbances and plague of hail; men blaspheme God

NOTES

1 BACKGROUND AND COMPOSITION OF THE NEW TESTAMENT

1. Others place the epistle later, about A.D. 62. If the early date is correct, it would give a date of only about fifteen years after the death of Christ.

3 GOSPEL OF JOHN

1. The most common words in the other Gospels are "powers" and "wonders." The former denotes the display of supernatural power in doing the miracle; the latter emphasizes the effect of the miracle upon the people—it left them awestruck.

4 BOOK OF ACTS

1. Chapter twelve is a glimpse into the persecution of some of the church leaders. James, the brother of John, was killed, and Peter was imprisoned. When released, Peter left the city, and James, the brother of Christ, became the leader of the Jerusalem church.

2. Between the record of the first and second journeys is the narrative of the Jerusalem Council. This council was occasioned by the teaching of certain men that the Gentiles must observe the Jewish law (cf. 15:19-21, 28, 29).

5 PAULINE EPISTLES: 1 AND 2 THESSALONIANS

1. The two prominent Rabbinical schools dated back to Hillel and Shammai. Hillel allowed his students greater freedom in their education, even to the reading of Greek writers.

2. Possibly Galatians 1:23 hints at a preaching ministry during these silent years, but the evidence is scant.

3. 1 Corinthians 5:9 indicates at least one such instance.

4. Although Galatians belongs in this group on the basis of its subject matter, it may well have been written earlier. Some place it as early as A.D. 48/49, others about A.D. 52/53. The date, however, does not affect its teaching.

5. The word translated "coming" in these passages literally meant "presence" in first-century usage (cf. 2 Cor. 10:10). But it also came to mean "arrival" and was used of the coming of a dignitary to some part of his domain.

6 PAULINE EPISTLES: 1 AND 2 CORINTHIANS

1. These are matters that relate to personal habits and scruples and for which Scripture allows liberty, i.e., habits of eating, dress, the use of time and such. See also Romans 14:1–15:13.

7 PAULINE EPISTLES: GALATIANS AND ROMANS

1. The Gospel came to him from Christ (1:12); he also has a new relationship to Christ (2:20).

2. The word *present* denotes an act of sacrifice; the words *be transformed* represent a process—a continual change from within. The latter is the basis for our English word *metamorphosis*.

8 THE PAULINE EPISTLES: COLOSSIANS, PHILEMON, EPHESIANS, PHILIPPIANS

1. "Put that to mine account" was a standard expression in bookkeeping in the first century. It referred to making an entry in the ledger. Sometimes the word is translated "reckon" (cf. Rom. 4:3-5).

2. Notice in this paragraph the repetition of the phrase "the praise of his glory" (1:6, 12, 14), distinguishing the work of the Father (v. 3-6), the Son (v. 7-12), and the Holy Spirit (v. 13, 14) in the creation of the Church.

3. In Colossians Paul gives most attention to the servant-master relationship (cf. Paul's let-
    ter to Philemon).
4. The term "wiles" (v. 11) is literally "strategy" or "methods" or "plans of attack." The
    companion expression, "fiery darts" (v. 16), refers to attacks of Satan upon the Christian.

9 PAULINE EPISTLES: 1 TIMOTHY, TITUS, 2 TIMOTHY

1. For a readable discussion, see D. Guthrie, *The Pastoral Epistles*, 11-52. A slightly more
    technical approach is taken by W. Hendricksen in *Exposition of the Pastoral Epistles*, 4-33.

10 THE CHURCH AND SUFFERING

1. The priestly and sacrificial system of the Old Testament (especially in the books of Exodus
    and Leviticus) forms the background for a proper understanding of Hebrews. This is par-
    ticularly true in 4:14–10:18. Christ is presented as the High Priest who has no successor
    (chap. 7), the mediator of the New Covenant which has no terminal point (chap. 8), and
    the spotless sacrifice who, by His once-for-all offering, has dealt with sin completely and
    finally (chap. 9 and 10).
2. See the outline for the character of each of the seven warnings.
3. The interpretation of these warning sections will be affected by the view one takes of the
    spiritual state of the recipients of the letter. Three major views are current: (1) they were
    only professing Christians, but never truly regenerated and were in danger of "stopping
    short of salvation"; (2) they were believers, but could lose salvation by failing to maintain
    faith in Christ; (3) they were believers who were in danger of lapsing into a life of barren-
    ness and uselessness, thus losing any reward.
4. It is also used with regard to Christ in 1:11; 2:21, 23; 3:18; 4:1, 13; 5:10—a total of seven
    times.
5. Notice also the occurrences of the word *grace* in the epistle—1:2, 10, 13; 2:19, 20;
    acceptable— 3:7; 4:10; *gift*—5:5, 10, 12.
6. There are over thirty such statements in this short epistle. See M. C. Tenney, *New Testament
    Survey,* rev. ed., 351, 352.

11 THE CHURCH AND FALSE TEACHING: 2 PETER, JUDE, 1, 2, AND 3 JOHN

1. The same word is used to characterize the redemptive work of Christ in Hebrews 9:12;
    10:10.
2. Jude also includes the devil as an example of blasphemy (v. 9, 10), although the incident
    is not included in any Old Testament book. It is taken from a Jewish intertestamental
    work and is used here as a graphic illustration of his characterization of the false teach-
    ers.
3. Even as the spoken word reveals the thought of the person, so the Lord Jesus revealed
    the Father (cf. John 1:18; 1 John 1:1, 2).
4. The former of these beliefs was called Docetism from the Greek word *dokeo,* "to seem (to
    be)"; the latter Cerinthianism, after the name of its champion, Cerinthus. Tradition informs
    us that John knew Cerinthus and regarded him as an enemy of the Gospel.

12 THE BOOK OF REVELATION

1. "The Letters to the Seven Churches of Asia" chart (page 105) will serve to present the char-
    acteristic words spoken by the Lord and the spiritual condition of each church.
2. Only these two among the seven cities are thriving communities today (although the
    names have been changed) and have maintained a Christian witness (Eastern Orthodox)
    in their locations. The Lord promised to each of them His protection and blessing because
    of their faithfulness (cf. John 17:15).
3. "The Three Series of Judgments" chart (page 106) gives a concise, consecutive analysis of
    the contents of each judgment. Reading it vertically will reveal the total impact of each
    series; reading it horizontally will show the contrasts and comparisons between each.
    This latter approach is especially important in relation to the trumpet and vial series.

BIBLIOGRAPHY

CHAPTER 1

Alexander, David and Pat, eds. *Eerdmans Handbook to the Bible*. Rev. ed. Grand Rapids: Eerdmans Publishing Co., 1983.

Bruce, F. F. *New Testament History*. Garden City, NY: Doubleday, 1972.

Gaebelein, Frank E., ed. *The Expositor's Bible Commentary: Vol. 1*. Grand Rapids: Zondervan Publishing House, 1979.

Geisler, N., and Nix, W. *From God to Us*. Chicago: Moody Press, 1974.

Halley, Henry H. *Halley's Bible Handbook*. Rev. ed. Grand Rapids: Zondervan Publishing House, 1976.

Metzger, B. M. *New Testament: Its Background, Growth and Content*. Nashville: Abingdon, 1979.

Morris, Leon., ed. *The Tyndale New Testament Commentary Series*. 20 vols. Grand Rapids: Eerdmans Publishing Co.

Scroggie, W. Graham. *A Guide to the Gospels*. Old Tappan, NJ: Fleming H. Revell Co. (Pickering & Inglis), 1975.

Tenney, Merrill C. *New Testament Survey*. Rev. ed. Grand Rapids: Eerdmans Publishing Co., 1985.

————. *New Testament Times*. Grand Rapids: Eerdmans Publishing Co., 1965.

Thomas, Robert L., and Gundry, Stanley N., eds. *A Harmony of the Gospels*. Chicago: Moody Press, 1978.

CHAPTER 2

Guthrie, Donald. *New Testament Introduction: Vol. 1*. Downers Grove, IL: InterVarsity Press, 1971.

Hunter, A. M. *The Parables Then & Now*. Philadelphia: Westminster Press, 1972.

Lane, William L. *Commentary on the Gospel of Mark*. Grand Rapids: Eerdmans Publishing Co., 1973.

Morris, Leon. *The Gospel According to St. Luke*. Grand Rapids: Eerdmans Publishing Co., 1974.

Stewart, J. S. *The Life & Teachings of Jesus Christ*. Nashville: Abingdon, 1982.

Thomas, Robert L., and Gundry, Stanley N. *A Harmony of the Gospels*. Chicago: Moody Press, 1978.

CHAPTER 3

Brown, R. E. *The Gospel According to John*. 2 vols. Garden City, NY: Doubleday, 1966, 1970.

Hendricksen, William. *John*. New Testament Commentary. Grand Rapids: Baker Book House, 1961.

Hunter, A. M. *Gospel According to John*. New York: Cambridge University Press, 1965.

Morris, Leon. *Gospel of John*. New International Commentary on the New Testament. Grand Rapids: Eerdmans Publishing Co., 1970.

Tenney, Merrill C. *John: The Gospel of Belief*. Grand Rapids: Eerdmans Publishing Co., 1948.

CHAPTER 4

Bruce, F. F. *The Book of the Acts*. New International Commentary on the New Testament. Grand Rapids: Eerdmans Publishing Co., 1954.

Longenecker, Richard. *Ministry & Message of Paul*. Grand Rapids: Zondervan Publishing House, 1971.

Vaughan, C. *Acts: A Study Guide Commentary*. Grand Rapids: Zondervan Publishing House, 1974.

CHAPTER 5

Bruce, F. F. *Paul: Apostle of the Heart Set Free*. Grand Rapids: Eerdmans Publishing Co., 1978.

Goodwin, Frank J. *A Harmony of the Life of St. Paul*. Grand Rapids: Baker Book House, 1964.

Hiebert, D. Edmond. *Thessalonian Epistles*. Chicago: Moody Press, 1971.

Morris, Leon. *First and Second Epistles to the Thessalonians*. New International Commentary on the New Testament. Grand Rapids: Eerdmans Publishing Co., 1959.

CHAPTER 6

Bruce, F. F. *Commentary on First & Second Corinthians*. The New Century Bible Commentary. Grand Rapids: Eerdmans Publishing Co., 1980.

Gaebelein, Frank E., ed. *The Expositor's Bible Commentary: Vol. 10*. Grand Rapids: Zondervan Publishing House, 1976.

Godet, Frederic L. *Commentary on First Corinthians*. Grand Rapids: Kregel Publications, 1977.

Hughes, Philip. *Commentary on the Second Epistle to the Corinthians*. Grand Rapids: Eerdmans Publishing Co., 1962.

CHAPTER 7

Moule, H. C. G. *Studies in Romans*. Grand Rapids: Kregel Publications, 1977.

Murray, John. *Epistle of Paul to the Romans*. 2 vols. New International Commentary on the New Testament. Grand Rapids: Eerdmans Publishing Co., 1960.

Tenney, Merrill C. *Galatians: The Charter of Christian Liberty*. Rev. ed. Grand Rapids: Eerdmans Publishing Co., 1960.

CHAPTER 8

Gaebelein, Frank E., ed. *The Expositor's Bible Commentary: Vol. 11*. Grand Rapids: Zondervan Publishing House, 1978.

Kent, Jr., Homer A. *Ephesians, the Glory of the Church*. Winona Lake, IN: BMH Books, 1971.

Moule, H. C. G. *Colossian and Philemon Studies*. Minneapolis: Klock & Klock, 1981.

_____. *Studies in Ephesians*. Grand Rapids: Kregel Publications, 1977.

_____. *Studies in Philippians*. Grand Rapids: Kregel Publications, 1977.

Muller, Jacobus J. *Epistles of Paul to the Philippians & Philemon*. New International Commentary on the New Testament. Grand Rapids: Eerdmans Publishing Co., 1961.

Simpson, E. K., and Bruce, F. F. *Epistles to the Ephesians and Colossians*. New International Commentary on the New Testament. Grand Rapids: Eerdmans Publishing Co., 1958.

CHAPTER 9

Kent, Jr., Homer A. *Pastoral Epistles*. Winona Lake, IN: BMH Books, 1982.

CHAPTER 10

Adamson, James B. *Commentary of the Epistle of James.* New International Commentary on the New Testament. Grand Rapids: Eerdmans Publishing Co., 1976.

Bruce, F. F. *The Epistle to the Hebrews.* New International Commentary on the New Testament. Grand Rapids: Eerdmans Publishing Co., 1964.

Kent, Jr., Homer A. *Epistle to the Hebrews.* Grand Rapids: Baker Book House, 1972.

Wiersbe, Warren W. *Be Mature.* Wheaton, IL: Victor Books, 1978.

CHAPTER 11

Boa, Kenneth. *Cults, World Religions, & You.* Wheaton, IL: Victor Books, 1977.

Breese, Dave. *Know the Marks of the Cults.* Wheaton, IL: Victor Books, 1975.

MacArthur, John, Jr. *Beware the Pretenders.* Wheaton, IL: Victor Books, 1980.

Marshall, I. H. *The New International Commentary on the New Testament: The Epistles of John.* Grand Rapids: Eerdmans Publishing Co., 1978.

Martin, Walter R. *The Kingdom of the Cults.* Rev. ed. Minneapolis, MN: Bethany Fellowship, 1985.

Wiersbe, Warren W. *Be Real.* Wheaton, IL: Victor Books, 1972.

CHAPTER 12

James, Edgar C. *The Day of the Lamb.* Wheaton, IL: Victor Books, 1980.

Ladd, G. E. *Commentary on the Book of Revelation of John.* Grand Rapids: Eerdmans Publishing Co., 1971.

Mounce, Robert H. *The Book of Revelation.* New International Commentary on the New Testament. Grand Rapids: Eerdmans Publishing Co., 1977.

Mounce, Robert H. *What Are We Waiting For?: A Commentary on Revelation.* Grand Rapids: Eerdmans Publishing Co., 1982.

Ryrie, C. C. *Revelation.* Chicago: Moody Press, 1968.

Tenney, Merrill C. *Interpreting Revelation.* Grand Rapids: Eerdmans Publishing Co., 1957.

Walvoord, John. *Revelation of Jesus Christ.* Chicago: Moody Press, 1966.